Craft from Natural Materials

Jane Bevan

With Photographs by Paul Tupman

  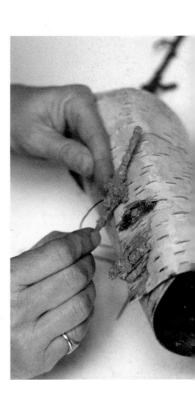

BLOOMSBURY

LONDON • NEW DELHI • NEW YORK • SYDNEY

**Dedicated to Dave, Alex, Oliver & Dan
And For Clare**

First published in Great Britain in 2013 by
Bloomsbury Publishing Plc
50 Bedford Square
London WC1B 3DP
www.bloomsbury.com

ISBN 978-1-4081-7087-8

All photos are by Paul Tupman unless
otherwise stated.

Book design: Elizabeth Healey
Cover design: Sutchinda Rangsi Thomson
Editor: Kate Sherington/Alison Stace

Printed and bound in China.

This book is produced using paper that is
made from wood grown in manageable,
sustainable forests. It is natural, renewable and
recyclable. The logging and manufacturing
processes conform to the environmental
regulations of the country of origin.

Right *Stick mobile, see p.56.*
Far right *Walking-stick maker Geoff Holt.*
Page 1 *Child's toy cricket from Tanzania,
made from leaves twisted together, 2005.
Private collection of Helen Juffs and Deirdre
Figueiredo.*

Frontispiece *Pine needle coiled basket,
Jane Bevan.*

Contents

Introduction

Scavenger: 'a person who searches for and collects discarded items'
Forage: 'obtain (food or provisions) by searching'

Above *Sycamore seed.*
Opposite, in clockwise direction from top
Clematis tendril, pine needles, animal bone, seed pod, shell, honesty seed, crab shell, feather, acorn, mussel shell.

This book is about going outside: to gather materials, to enjoy the outdoors and to make lasting and unique artworks. It is for everyone who is a bit in awe of nature. Whether you are new to making art, or more experienced, you will hopefully find new ideas, challenges and inspiration among the projects in this book.

How often have you returned from a walk with a feather, conker or special leaf in your coat pocket? So often these 'finds' end up forgotten in your pocket or a drawer, and just occasionally make it to the mantelpiece. If that sounds familiar, then this might be the book for you! With a little time and enthusiasm you can use these materials to make long-lasting artworks, souvenirs of a walk in the woods, a day on the beach or a picnic in the local park.

I always come back from a walk with some new treasure stashed in my back pocket. It might be a feather, a bit of lamb's wool, a stick or a leaf – every day seems to offer up something new. I have always loved to collect: anything from fruit stickers to snow globes, seaside souvenirs to beach pebbles. There is an enormous amount of pleasure to be gained in finding a new item for your collection – a beautiful, unspoilt piece of birch bark or a bright red autumn leaf. Beachcombing at any age is also a delight. There is no predicting what you will find and you will rarely be disappointed! These pleasures are free and wonderful outdoor pastimes for when you are alone, as well as with family and children.

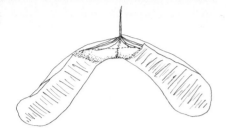

Above Sycamore seeds, often referred to as helicopters or whirlybirds, are much loved, especially by children. Drawing by Dan, aged 8½.

Opposite Necklace from Brazil made from seeds threaded together, bird feathers and a beetle wing pendant, 1999. Private collection of Helen Juffs and Deirdre Figueiredo. Photo: Paul Tupman.

Below Amazonian Shuttlecock from Brazil, made from macaw feathers, 1999. Private collection of Helen Juffs and Deirdre Figueiredo. Photo: Paul Tupman.

There is an innate collector in us all, and from childhood onwards we are drawn to picking up and sorting materials. What we must do is learn to value these materials more. They are not 'just a bit of rubbish', but intricately designed fragments of nature, perfect in their colours, patterns and functions.

My favourite is the sycamore seed, designed to catch the wind and rotate through the air, taking it far enough away from the parent tree to root. Nature working at its best!

I know I am not alone in these pleasures and, along with many other people, feel a great affinity with the countryside and the woodlands of England. If we ask ourselves how this fascination grows, it is perhaps through the literature and films of our childhood. From the warmth and romance of the tales of *Robin Hood* to *The Children of the New Forest* by Edward Marryat, the forest in literature has been represented as a haven – a safe and exciting place to hide. Other literary landscapes that might have contributed to my attachment are the wintery, desolate, Essex marshes of *The Snow Goose* by Paul Gallico and the rural homelands or Shires of *The Hobbit* by J. R. R Tolkien. You may be thinking of many more straight away that apply to your own beloved environments.

Before moving on to start collecting and making, it is worth taking a moment to consider the global and historical context for making with natural materials. Throughout history, people have used natural materials because there was nothing else. Everything that was needed in the home and for work could be woven, knitted, sewn or constructed using local materials, whether bought, exchanged or found. By the 20th century, recycling, for many people, was a way of life, out of necessity or a reluctance to

waste anything. Tools, clothes, shoes, furniture and toys would all be mended many times over and buying things new was rare.

Making with natural materials is a little like going back to basics, re-examining what we need and use in our lives. Do we want to be always surrounded by coloured, cheap plastics and machine-made objects, or can we let more nature and simplicity back into our lives?

A trip to a museum such as the Pitt Rivers Museum in Oxford or the British Museum in London will offer inspiration and a chance to see the incredible, preserved artefacts of this history. Museums are full of these treasures, from baskets, jewellery and toys to birch-bark shoes and boats, all demonstrating the universal innovation and resourcefulness of people using the natural materials around them.

Above *Interior of the Pitt Rivers Museum, University of Oxford, Oxford. The Pitt Rivers Museum is a vasl treasure house, full of innovative objects made from natural materials across the centuries and around the world. Photo: Jane Bevan, used with permission of the Pitt Rivers Museum.*

How to use this book: practical advice

THE PROJECTS

Each of the 12 separate projects in this book introduces new materials, new techniques and new ideas, so you will end up with a rich variety of handmade artworks. Each project can be further developed by using alternative materials or experimenting with size and shape. There is no order to the projects; dip in as you wish, depending on which takes your fancy on any given day. As you find materials and work with them, you will begin to form a real bond with your work. Wherever you are in the world, whether in town or in the country, there will be some suitable materials, so look closely and experiment with what you find. Trying anything new is daunting and getting started is undoubtedly the hardest part!

Designing and making with natural, unrefined materials, such as leaves, twigs and bark, brings new and different challenges. Although the projects in this book suggest particular 'tried and tested' methods of working, it is still difficult to predict exactly what the materials will best respond to. Try to keep an open mind about the final result and work out what the materials want to do, adapting your ideas as you go along. It might be by twisting, plaiting or some other technique that you will get the most pleasing results. It is so much better to allow the materials to work in their own way rather than fight against them, even if it means not sticking

The techniques used in the featured projects are shown here. These are simple and traditional techniques that have been used for centuries across the world. The techniques are explained in the book, but can also be read about in a number of other books (see Further Reading, p.89), on the internet (see Websites, p.90) and instructional videos viewed on YouTube.

TECHNIQUES

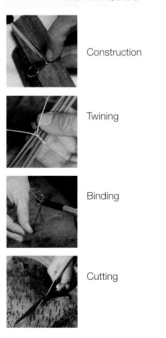

Construction

Twining

Binding

Cutting

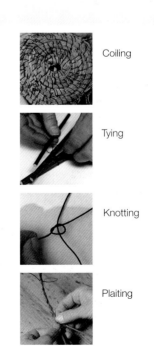

Coiling

Tying

Knotting

Plaiting

to your original plan. Dr Tim Willey, sculptor, craftsman and applied ecologist, introduces artists to this adaptive learning approach through his teaching and writing (see www.timwilley.com).

The more making you do, the better you will get and the more flexible and dexterous your fingers will become. People like to say they are 'all fingers and thumbs' but that feeling will pass when you warm up, start making and begin to unlock your creativity.

The projects are designed to use only basic and simple hand tools, such as hammer and nails, screwdriver, needle and thread, scissors and secateurs – items that you may already have in your tool box, or that can be easily and cheaply purchased from hardware shops.

WORKING CONDITIONS

You won't need a studio or a separate room to work in; the kitchen table will be fine. I work on a number of large trays that can easily be moved out of the way when necessary. I guarantee you will already have worked with similar materials in your home environment – perhaps you have carved out a Halloween pumpkin, made a daisy chain or helped to construct a den in the garden.

PRESERVING ARTWORK

If kept in dry conditions, your new artworks will last many years and there is no need to treat them further. Just an occasional dust or wipe with a wet cloth will suffice. Some materials, however, such as reeds and leaves, will dry out and shrivel slightly. Don't be put off by this – it is part of the joy of the materials, as the colours, textures and even smells will change slowly over time.

TIME

I have given the approximate time that each project takes to make (not including collecting time). You may, of course, decide not to finish the project in one go, but to return to it over a period of time. Either way, do allow yourself enough time when starting a project. It can be frustrating when you are interrupted too often, and the benefit of spending time totally absorbed in your work, may be lost. These projects take care and concentration, but can also be extremely relaxing, and wonderful for feeling calm and at ease. I like to think of making art as part of the Slow Movement, (www.theslowmovement.com), a reaction to the fast pace of life so many of us lead these days. The Movement shows us how to reconnect with the world around us, leading a more meaningful and balanced life, whether it is through travel, food, communities, lifestyle or making art.

Above Mask-making workshop led by artist Dr Tim Willey at Mattishall Primary School, Norfolk, 2012. Photo: Dr Tim Willey.

Getting Started

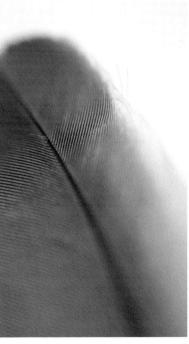

Materials

Where to find materials

Of the 12 projects in this book, several do require wire or waxed thread, and a little glue might help occasionally, but most of the materials used can be found outdoors and occur naturally. Thorns, twigs, bark and branches can be tough, durable and long-lasting, and silver birch bark, leaves, acorn cups, feathers, pebbles and beachcombed material provide a rich palette of resources to work from.

Materials can be found in your garden, local parks, school playing fields or even on the street. Nature creeps in everywhere if you start to look closely. You might also explore beach and coastal areas, river bank, lake side, canal and woodlands. Just keep your eye to the ground and your imagination alive.

There is a great deal to be said for getting to know and love what is on your doorstep. Study the changing seasons in your garden, park or local beauty spot and you will develop a new understanding and love of the great outdoors. As the seasons change you will see new colours, shapes and materials to admire and there will always be the anticipation of the next stage. Just one horse chestnut tree can, throughout the year, provide beautiful leaves, conkers, flowers and strong, reddish stems, which can be used in a variety of ways.

Above *Birch twigs gathered to make a broom.*

Background *Autumn in Charnwood. Photo: Terry Davies.*

GARDENS

Whether you live in the city or countryside, nature will be pushing its way through if you just look closely enough. Start with your own or a neighbour's garden; you will be surprised at the wide range of materials to be found there, from pine needles and grass to rose brambles, twigs or thorns. Urban gardens are extremely important for the health and wellbeing of all of us, but due to pressure on space, many front and back gardens have been increasingly paved over for cars and property development. In London front gardens, the equivalent of 5,200 football pitches have been lost in recent years. This impacts on insects and wildlife, adds to flash flooding, and worsens the effects of climate change. There is a wonderful campaign in Britain to preserve front gardens, which you can follow on the Royal Horticultural Society website and perhaps encourage in your own neighbourhood (see www.rhs.org.uk/Gardening/Sustainable-gardening/pdfs/FrontGardens).

PARKS

If your garden doesn't contain enough material, the next stop might be your local park. Urban parks are a key feature of most cities around the world and provide green spaces that are crucial to our wellbeing, for both physical activity and mental rest. London is one of the greenest capital cities in the world, with more than 3,000 public parks and open spaces in the city. There you will find leaves, seeds, conkers and acorns in abundance.

Above Wherever you are in a city, town or village, you will never be far from a public footpath.

Below In one day, 40 people collected 40 kg of marine litter from the beach, including 340 caps/lids, 391 rope pieces, 1,661 pieces of plastic, 4 toothbrushes and 35 shotgun cartridges, possibly from across the Atlantic. Watergate Bay, North Cornwall Beach Clean-Up Day, 2011. Photo: Amy Marsh.

THESE ARE SOME BASIC RULES TO FOLLOW WHEN YOU ARE OUT

- Always ask permission from the landowner to collect materials.
- Do not pick flowers or living plants of any kind.
- Do not disturb living plants or animals.
- Do not collect in a nature reserve or conservation area.
- Only take what materials you need.
- Pick up materials from the ground only if you think it is safe to do so and use rubber gloves if necessary
- Leave no trace of your visit and clear up litter before you leave – even if it isn't yours.
- Keep dogs under control.
- Respect other people using the area.
- Leave gates closed and property as you find it and follow paths unless wider access is clearly permitted.
- If you are going off alone consider telling someone where you are heading and take a phone with you.
- When you are back home, wash your hands carefully!

Above On a foraging outing in the woods. Be prepared to tell people what you are up to. There is always lots of curiosity from passers-by when you are out collecting.

OPEN COUNTRYSIDE

You may want to travel further to broaden your foraging possibilities and there are plenty of locations to choose from. In Britain, you are never far from an area of woodland, forest, open countryside, moorland, canal towpath or reservoir. There are also public footpaths in every village and town, taking walkers through privately owned farmland on permitted paths. In North America, Australia and the rest of Europe, there are similar areas of natural beauty, rich in materials for your pieces. However, do not forget that all land belongs to someone, so do not trespass and always ask permission to take materials. Even then, only take small amounts for your own personal use. The rules are different for conservation areas and Sites of Special Scientific Interest, which are areas to look at and admire only. Always ask permission and, in the UK, follow the Countryside Code – which will be helpful to consider everywhere (see www.naturalengland.org.uk/ourwork/enjoying/countrysidecode). See other useful websites on p. 90.

BEACHES

The beach, too, is a great place to walk, hunt for materials, picnic and relax in the fresh air. In Britain, beachcombing can be more rewarding in winter, before the beach has been cleaned up for the tourists, and after the stormy weather has passed. Beaches near an industrial area or large city can often be littered with fascinating non-natural materials, such as plastics, fishing debris and sea glass. Beachcombers can do a great service by picking up some of this litter and helping to keep beaches clean. It can be great fun to join a Beach Clean group, often organised at the start of the summer season. Material is collected and sorted, and research sent to the UK Marine Conservation Society for use in their campaign for cleaner beaches (see www.sas.org.uk/campaigns/marine-litter).

Benefits of foraging outdoors

There is a great deal of research to show that spending time outside, particularly amongst the trees, is a huge boost to our physical and mental health, reducing stress, encouraging exercise and helping us to feel more in touch with nature. You don't need to be super-fit or sporty either, there are many social groups you can join for walking at any age, from mums and toddlers to older generations. You can even sign up to a guided nature walk to learn about wildlife and plants, from bats and moths to orchids and trees. Look on the internet or ask at your local library for information.

Whenever the countryside becomes threatened by development, destruction or by a fungal disease, such as Chalara ash dieback currently threatening ash trees across Europe, we see enthusiastic national campaigns that reflect how connected people feel to the countryside. When you are working closely with nature, you cannot fail to be moved by the issues affecting it, so add your voice to the crowd!

Collecting and gathering

When you have decided to begin collecting materials, prepare a bag, ideally a backpack, and take your secateurs, knife, camera, sketchbook and pencils with you.

I often wish I had an extra pair of hands and if it is getting dark early I have been known to wear a head torch to help me see and keep my hands free! Within reason, set out whatever the weather – if we wait for a sunny day, it may never happen – and take all you need with you. You will undoubtedly be out longer than expected.

Time spent outdoors in the woods, in the park or on the beach is invigorating, and it is always a challenge to find new materials. Don't discard anything that attracts your attention – take it home and spend time thinking what you might do with it.

When beachcombing, it is worth remembering to take a mobile phone and check the local weather and tides. Take care on slippery rocks, do not climb on the cliffs, and do not disturb any living plants and animals.

Storage and display of materials

When you have collected a range of fascinating natural items, from poppy seed heads to sycamore seeds and leaves, it would be a shame to hide them away until you are ready to use them. So in the meantime, why not put them on display? Have a look through some of the monthly house and lifestyle magazines, they are full of ideas for display in the home.

Displaying these materials may remind you of your school nature table, when found treasures, from birds' nests to pine cones, were laid out thoughtfully for everyone to see, with handwritten labels and careful items of research. Nature tables are less common in schools now, despite the many benefits. Why not get any youngsters you know involved? They could suggest to teachers that they start one at their school.

A handy tip is if you wish to prolong the green stage before materials dry out, then try artist Anna King's advice. She stores her materials in the freezer in labelled bags so she can have fresh green pine needles at any time of year.

Below and opposite *Display materials on shelves, on a mantelpiece or sort them into labelled glass jars.*

Below right *Try drilling small holes into a length of wood (with a flat side to rest on) and storing individual feathers in the holes. They will look stunning in a window with the light shining through.*

Sketchbooks and Journals

A really important and fulfilling part of making any sort of art is keeping a sketchbook or journal as you go along. If you prefer it can be a totally private book, just for you, and it will help enormously to develop ideas, gather information, and jog your memory when you come to make the work. With sketchbook in hand, you may feel a little self-conscious at first, but as you get quicker and more confident, you will wonder how you ever managed without it. It will give you huge pleasure looking back over it in time.

When you are going out collecting, it would be a good idea to take a small camera as well as your sketchbook, pencils, pencil sharpener and maybe charcoal with you. Standard pencils are fine, but you might also want to experiment with harder and softer pencils, fibre tipped pens and crayons. A small watercolour set with brush and water fitted inside is excellent for working outdoors.

When you are out, it is better to sketch quickly and freely without worrying about quality – take a rug or a folding chair if you will be out sometime, otherwise you can always finish the drawing later and add colour back at home. If you are in a hurry or the weather is really bad, then take quick photos and use them to draw from later.

Most artists use sketchbooks and there are some beautiful examples that will give you ideas, such as the drawings of Cezanne, Henry Moore and David Hockney, which you might find in your local library, online or in specialist bookshops.

As well as the sketchbook, you might also like to start a nature journal or diary, making a note of the materials you see and when in the year they are available. You can also add bits of research and notes to help you remember any ideas. I love the idea of writing just one sentence a day, no more. Being limited to a small amount is much less daunting and looking back it has been really useful to focus on what is important.

Above Chris Drury, Medicine Wheel, *16th August 1982–15th August 1983. One natural object for each day of the year. Twelve segments of paper, one for each month, were made during that month from the pulp of particular plants, 230 x 8 cm (90 x 3 in.). Held in the collection of the Leeds City Art Gallery. Photo: Chris Drury.*

Below Choose a sketchbook with a good, hard cover to last longer, and that is small enough to fit easily in your pocket or bag.

Mini research projects

- In early spring, find a cherry blossom tree just before it breaks into blossom. Take a photograph every day, following how the colour develops, reaches its peak and then dies away. You can take the photographs at exactly the same time each day or go back at different times. These photographs would look fascinating framed up in a line or stapled into a small flip-book.

- Select an interesting patch of the ground in the woods. Take a bird's eye view photograph of the patch of ground, in each of the four seasons, showing the changing vegetation, leaves, colours and light on the often-overlooked floor.

- Hedgerows are wonderfully dense and complex ecosystems, home to plants, animals, birds and insects. In Britain some hedges are more than 700 years old. Make an in-depth study of a particular section of nearby hedgerow with a range of plant species. Study it carefully and try to identify the plants. Make sketches, line drawings and watercolours. Take photographs

throughout the year to show how it changes through the seasons.

- Make a temporary artwork that is not intended to last. It can be very rewarding, and you can preserve the memory of it through a photograph or in your sketchbook. It could be a giant spiral of stones on the beach, autumn leaves threaded onto wire, or a tower of stones precariously balanced.

- Select a few very colourful autumn leaves and laminate them. You will be amazed how long the colour will last. Cut them out, tie string through a small hole at the top, and hang them outside from a sparse tree in winter for decoration.

Below and right Each section of a hedge contains a rich array of plant and wildlife. The plants make a dense pattern of interlocking branches, reminiscent of random basketry. Photos: Jane Bevan

Three useful skills

There are a number of simple, traditional skills used in this book, but the three most useful – sewing, knotting and twining – are worth introducing at the beginning as a warm-up exercise.

----

1. SEWING

Sewing is done with a needle and thread, usually to attach two items together. Needles were used thousands of years ago by the Romans and were made of bone and wood. Today you can buy a wide range – wedge needles for leather (these are good for bark too) with a triangular point designed not to tear the material; heavy, long upholstery needles; curved needles for awkward places such as the inside of a vessel; and tapestry needles with a larger eye for thicker yarn.

If you want to treat yourself and really enjoy the tools of your work, visit Merchant and Mills Drapers' shops, or check them out online (http://merchantandmills.com). They have a very stylish range of haberdashery items, beautifully packaged and available online and in various shops worldwide (see p. 88 for details). I have also managed to buy sewing tools very cheaply at markets, charity shops and even car boot sales.

There are a number of different stitches you can use, including running, back, cross, blanket and chain stitch. When using natural materials choose a stitch that will be strong enough for the job but do keep stitches to a minimum, especially if your materials are delicate, such as a leaf or bark.

For more help and ideas on sewing, visit the Embroiderers Guild website: www.embroiderersguild.com/stitch.

Above Susanna Bauer, Spring, 2012. Magnolia leaf with cotton yarn crochet, 9 x 5 cm (3½ x 2 in). Photo: Susanna Bauer.

Above The running stitch (top image) is the basic stitch on which all others are based. The stitch is made by passing the needle in and out of the material. Running stitches may be of varying lengths and are very quick to make. Back stitches (bottom image) form a solid line and are made by sewing in small stitches against the direction of sewing.

Far left Using needle and waxed thread to start the pine needle basket (see p.65).

Left Attaching a small twig (or toggle) as if sewing on a button.

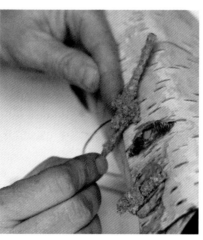

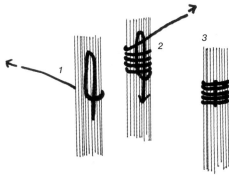

2. KNOTTING

Most people learn to tie only a few knots in their lifetime and often that might be enough. It is a great skill, however, to have more, so take some time out and teach yourself some useful knots from books or the internet. YouTube is excellent for animated knot demonstrations and many of these will be useful when you are making with natural materials. The whipping knot is a very tidy way to secure bundles together, very useful for reeds and grasses.

Common Whipping Knot

1 Make a bight (loop) with the cord along the length of the reeds. With the left-hand end, begin to wrap around the reeds, securely trapping the bight.

2 Slip the end of the cord through the bight and hold. Pull on the opposite loose end until the bight is inside and hidden by the cord.

3 Cut the cord flush at both ends for a neat finish.

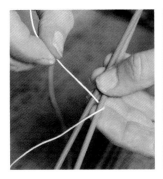 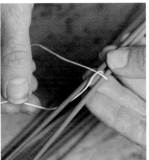 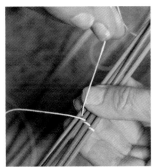 

3. TWINING

Twining is one of the oldest and most popular basketry techniques, particularly suitable for soft materials such as reeds and grasses.

Two lengths of thread (weavers) are woven around the spokes or uprights (in this case, reeds). The weavers cross over between the uprights for a half turn or for a full turn. Either style is fine as long as you are consistent. Twining is a simple process and relaxing to do, but also requires some concentration to keep the weave even and regular.

If there is a gap between the spokes on view, then it is called space twining. If the twining is pulled tight to close the gap, it is called close twining and takes considerably longer. It is a very popular technique due to the patterns that can be made and the overall strength it gives the structure.

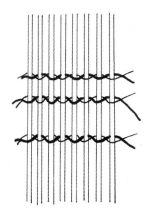

Projects

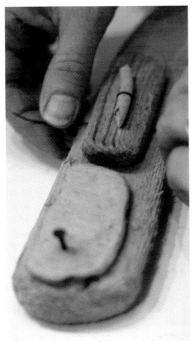

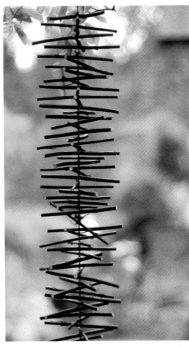

Nature picture

Materials:

- Box frame (from Ikea or a framing shop) with a fitted cardboard mount
- Piece of card 14 x 14 cm (5½ x 5½ in)
- Acorn cups
- Beeswax or linseed oil
- Wood glue or PVA glue
- Masking tape

Tools:

- Tweezers
- Thin paintbrush
- Cloth
- Sandpaper

Some of the natural materials you will discover on walks are so small, and so perfect in their own way, that the best use is to frame them up and admire them daily on your wall. Here, nature can be seen as art in its own right – a seed head or wild clematis tendril can become a picture as worthy of admiration and contemplation as any painting.

The tiny woody cup from the base of an acorn is a perfectly formed natural gem, with its rough casing and smooth, ringed interior. They may have played a part in your childhood play – I know I used them as fairy boats, hats and soup bowls once or twice!

COLLECTING AND MAKING

Easy to find in woods or parks, the acorn cup can be found on the ground from autumn right through until early spring. If you are in a field, you may find that cows often lie around the base of the tree and crush the cups, so try looking a little way away from the tree for the best examples. Select the largest ones with few cracks and don't worry about the dirt, they will clean up really well. You may want to use rubber gloves if the ground is particularly wet or dirty.

Once you are home, you can begin cleaning the acorns and putting together your unique nature picture.

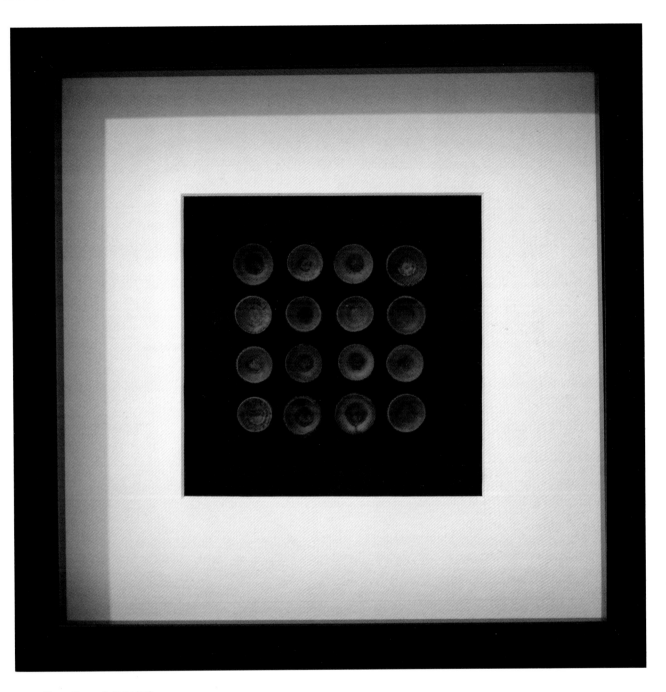

Above *Generally items look better laid out in rows, with space between to appreciate the shapes.*

Left *Keep a box of 'spare' pieces of nature and when it is full you can put together a picture like this.*

1 Wash the acorns you wish to use and remove any acorn stalks by hand. 16 is a good number to use in a grid pattern.

2 Place the acorn cups individually on sandpaper on the table, and sand down the bases until they sit flat.

3 Wax or oil the interiors using beeswax to enhance the colours, or for a darker finish, use linseed oil dabbed on with a thin paintbrush or cloth.

4 On a piece of black card cut to fit the mount, position the cups in a grid pattern. It is a fiddly job, so it may help to use tweezers when moving the objects around. When you are happy with the positioning, glue them down using a thin paintbrush and a very small amount of glue. Ideally leave them overnight, or for at least four hours to allow them to dry fully.

5 Use masking tape to fix the card onto the mount from the back. Make sure the picture is central in the mount. Clean the glass in the frame really well, place your artwork on its mount into the frame, and seal it up, following the manufacturer's instructions.

6 Mount the frame onto the wall or leave free standing on a shelf.

IDEAS FOR EXTRA TIME

If acorn cups are not available, you can frame just about anything, from flat slate stones and sycamore seeds, to pine-tree scales and clematis tendrils. In the southern hemisphere, you might use the gum nut, which can be found all year round.

Below Picture made from mixed nature finds from the woods.
Right Marian Bijlenga, Written Weed, *2004. Fern collage number 101, 42 x 31 cm (16½ x 12 in). From a limited edition book, each collage is made from natural materials and is meticulously arranged, acting as a moment of contemplation and a reminder of the place. Photo: Marian Bijlenga.*

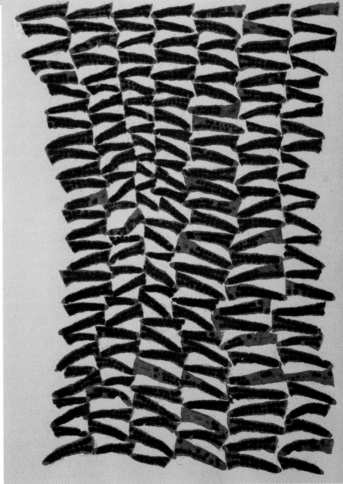

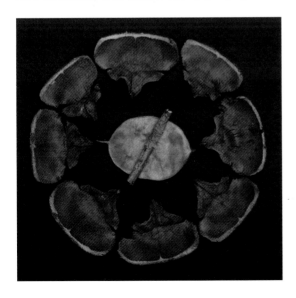

Slate cluster pendant

Materials:
- Small, thin pieces of slate from the beach
- Shells
- Leather or cotton thread 100 cm (39½ in) long

Tools:
- Hand drill
- Blu-tack
- Scissors
- Protective facemask when drilling slate
- Eye protectors
- Tin snips

Natural pebbles and stones make beautiful pendants, not least because they warm up in the sun and feel wonderful against your skin. This project is a cheap and easy way to make a really unique, inexpensive and special piece of jewellery.

COLLECTING AND MAKING

When collecting pieces of slate, look for interesting shapes and choose very thin pieces that can be drilled easily. Collect a few more than you will need as some will inevitably crack in the process. Although rocks and pebbles can be found in all types of urban and rural environments, I prefer to use stones found on the beach, which are already beautifully smooth after being tossed around for so long by the sea.

SAFETY TIP

The dust from slate is not good for you, so wear a face mask for this part. Clean the dust away carefully and wash your hands well when you're done. Wash and dry the stone before proceeding.

Right and opposite Unique pendants to wear, or give as a gift, using slate and found beach plastic.

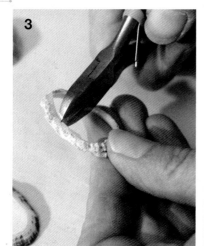

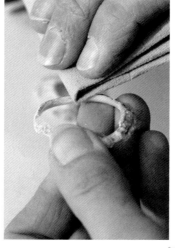

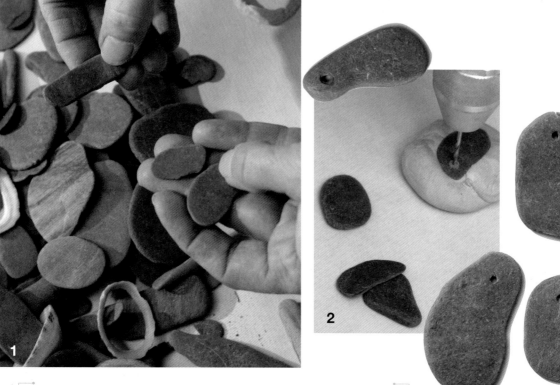

drill with a 2.0 mm drill bit. The hole needs to be just big enough to thread the cord through. If you prefer a polished look the slate is soft enough to sand with sandpaper. Personally I like to stay with the shapes as I have found them, keeping them as natural as possible.

3 Add other materials if you wish – anything that you can drill through, such as tiny pieces of driftwood or rings of shell.

To make shell rings, use a shell that is already damaged on the top, or crack it open at the top carefully with a hammer. Using tin snips, gently snip away from the inside until you have a thin outer ring. Wearing eye protectors is essential, as tiny pieces of shell will shoot away in the process. I hate to say but this job is very much like cutting your toe nails – a delicate and rather unpleasant operation!

1 When you have the stones home, wash them and play around for a while with the shapes. Do you want a cluster of stones for your pendant, or just one or two?

2 Secure the slate to be drilled onto a large lump of blu-tack fixed to the table. This will be enough to keep it still while you drill if you don't have a small vice. I am using a simple hand

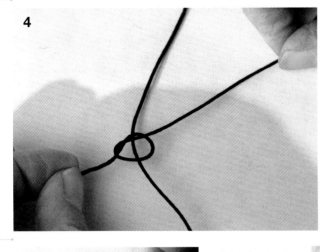

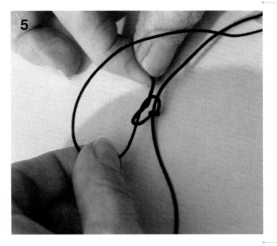

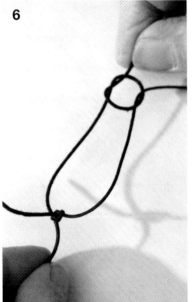

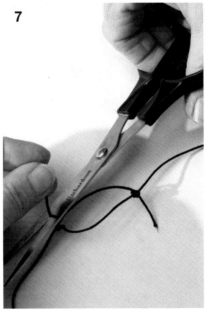

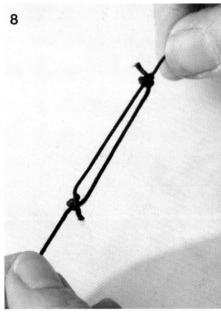

4 To prepare the cord, cut 80 cm (31½ in) of leather or cotton thread. Tie it with a sliding knot so you can alter the length to suit you. First tie a loose half-knot with one end and feed the opposite end through, pulling the knot tight to trap it inside.

5 Repeat to make a double knot. Then thread 4 to 6 slate pieces onto the cord.

6 Go to the other end of the cord and tie a second knot.

7 Trim the ends.

8 Adjust the sliding knot to fit.

Driftwood fish sculpture

How often do you come home from the beach with treasured pieces of driftwood but no idea what to do with them? Here is one project to use up your beach material and make a shoal of wall-mounted fish, perfect for a bathroom or outside wall, as a souvenir of a holiday or day out.

Materials:

- Numerous small pieces of driftwood
- Cuttlebone, shells, crab claws or similar for decoration
- Bird feathers
- Waxed thread
- Garden wire
- D-ring for hanging
- Beeswax or linseed oil if required

Tools:

- Hand drill
- Scissors
- Bradawl or sharp pointed tool
- Sandpaper
- Knife
- Glue
- Hammer
- Rubber gloves or a litter picker

Note:

- You will only need simple tools for this project which you may already have or can be purchased at a low cost.

COLLECTING AND MAKING

Collecting the driftwood is a big part of this project. Try to just take what you need and leave some for everyone else! Some beaches will have more driftwood than others. You will likely find more in the winter months, after a storm, or on a wilder, more windswept coast, where material may have travelled great distances from across the ocean.

Collect pieces of wood that you like the look of, in a variety of sizes and shapes. Look out for oddities or quirks reminiscent of animal features in the wood, such as 'eyes', rusty nails and segments of old paint. Sort through the debris deposited at the tide line, the highest point where the waves reach, and look for small pieces that may be tucked away under seaweed and the inevitable plastic bags and rubbish. Use rubber gloves or a litter picker if you are rummaging in the heaps of beach debris and be very careful what you pick up.

Try not to worry too much about the rather fishy smell but do ensure to wash your hands really well at the end.

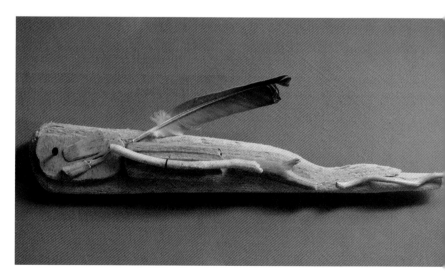

Above *A wall-mounted driftwood fish.*

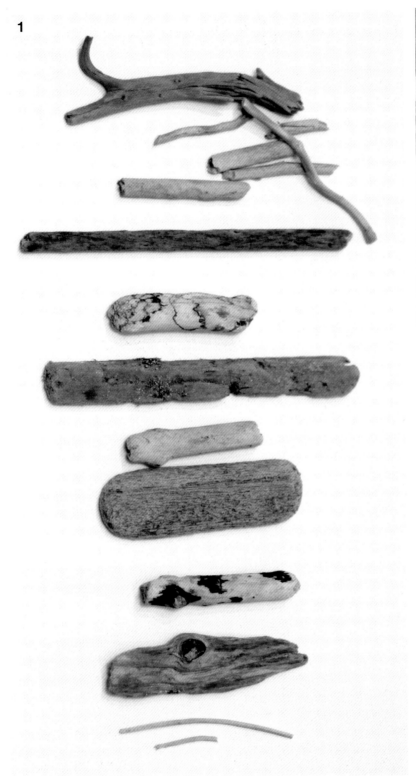

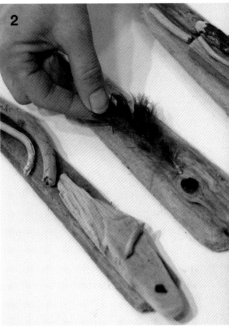

1 Back at home, sort through your pieces of wood and spend time moving them around on a surface and playing with ideas. Can you see a fish or a bird shape, maybe a fantasy creature? Children are often very good at spotting shapes so ask for help from family if you can.

2 Start off with more pieces of wood than you need, as you will reject and maybe break pieces as you go along. Move the pieces around, layer them on top of each other and lay out your design on the table.

You could carve the wood with a penknife if it is very soft or shave pieces off to suit. Always cut away from you and put the blade away carefully when not in use.

3

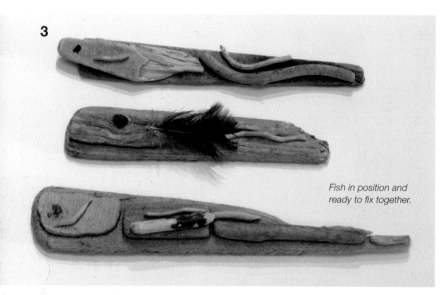

3 Once the shape is decided, you can begin to attach pieces together. My particular pieces of wood in this example, from North Cornwall, seemed to suggest fish shapes, so I have made a shoal of three fish. There are a variety of ways to fix driftwood together. Large pieces can be nailed with hammer and nails, whereas smaller pieces can be wired, tied with thread or string, or even glued. Where possible, try to make the fixings part of the design. For example, the nail can become the fish eye and the thread forms patterns on the fish's back.

Fish in position and ready to fix together.

4

5

4 Drill a hole through the soft driftwood with a hand drill and pull the waxed thread through, for tying together as tightly as possible. Decide if you want to treat the wood and change its appearance by sanding down to create a smoother finish, waxing, or treating with linseed oil to make the wood darker.

5 To make an eye, break off a small piece of cuttlebone, carve gently with a knife to an oval shape, and glue on. Carefully glue on other features with a thin paintbrush. It will be possible to simply tuck in extra features, such as a feather, at the end.

6 If the fish are to be wall mounted, first make a small hole with a bradawl into the back of the fish, in the middle and low down enough to be hidden from the front. Then attach a D-ring with a screw into the hole. You can hook this onto a nail inside, or on an outside garden wall.

Below Karen Miller, Angel Fish, 2010. Driftwood collected from beaches on the North American West Coast, 50 x 60 cm (19½ x 24 in). Karen Miller lives in Devon and has been designing and creating driftwood art for over a decade. She is as captivated by the driftwood now as when she first started. Photo: Karen Miller.

Beach faces

There is so much more to beachcombing than just driftwood. The beach offers a wide range of fascinating bits and pieces, perfect for an art project, and so often completely overlooked!

Materials:
- One fairly large driftwood stick, 30 cm (12 in) or longer
- Range of natural beach debris, such as shells, driftwood, cuttlebones, seaweed and assorted driftwood pieces
- Man-made debris, such as plastics, broken toys, metals, rope and sea glass

Tools:
- Rubber gloves or litter picker/ pick-up tool
- Glue
- Wire
- Hammer and nails
- String
- Scissors
- Wire cutters

Wherever you are in the world there will be a wealth of natural and man-made materials washed up along the coastline. You can use seaweed, shells, cuttlebones and stones, but also add some man-made marine litter too. Plastics, corks, broken toys, coloured string, fishing line and hooks, glass and other abandoned materials wash up on beaches, causing problems for wildlife and fishing. Plastic is not biodegradable and will degrade even slower in the marine environment than on land. This means that a normal plastic bottle may sit for more than 450 years if left on a beach.

So this is one project where a little man-made material will really add to the look of your piece, and help clean up the beach at the same time. Most importantly, be very careful what debris you pick up and supervise children closely. Use plastic gloves or even a litter picker and try to avoid anything sharp or not easily identifiable. Report anything out of the ordinary to the authorities.

COLLECTING AND MAKING

If you are travelling, you may want to seal the finds in a tight plastic bag to stop any smell escaping until you get home! Wash hands well afterwards and clean up your materials in hot soapy water, preferably outside.

This project will depend on what you have found on the beach. For example, after a stormy weekend in West Dorset, I found more than 30 cuttlebones in a very small area and similarly, on a Lincolnshire beach, thousands of razor clams on one day. Only use discarded or washed-up material and never touch living creatures or plants.

Whatever you find you will be able to create an interesting artwork by experimenting and playing with your materials.

Left & Opposite Beach masks made of rope, plastics, roots, driftwood, seaweed, an old gun cartridge from North America, mussel shells, comb, toothbrush, bottle tops and the base of a metal can.

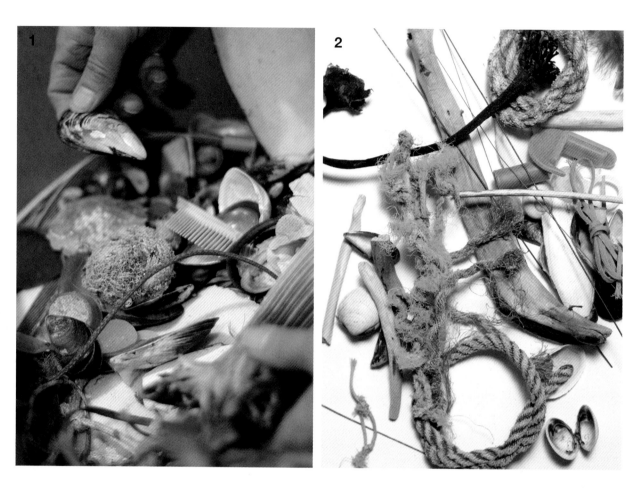

1 On a tabletop, lay out your materials including big and small pieces and at least one larger piece of driftwood 30 cm (12 in) long.

2 Taking your time, start to move items around. Here we have fishing string, cuttlebone, mussel shells, seaweed, plastics, driftwood, feathers and rope. Layer some on top of each other and play with the shapes and sizes. Can you spot facial features and the makings of a mask, such as a nose, beard, hair, mouth, eyes or ears?

3 Use the large piece of driftwood as your starting point. When you have features sorted out, try different means of attaching items to each other. You can nail together larger pieces of wood, wire plastics together loosely, glue shells, and knot or tie on pieces of string and seaweed.

4 To hang the finished faces, knock two small nails into the wall, just wide enough to go either side of the main driftwood. The mask will then rest on the nails.

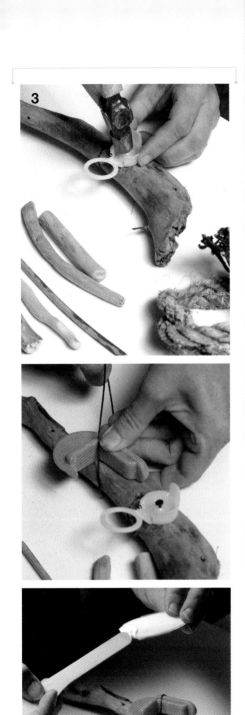

3

4

Birch bark tea-light holder

Materials:

- One rectangular piece of silver birch bark, 25 x 10 cm (10 x 4 in)
- Clean glass jam jar or tin can, 10 cm high x 6 cm diameter (4 x 2½ in)
- Waxed thread or cord, 20 cm (8 in) long
- Stick, seed or pebble to use as a toggle (elongated button), 2 cm (¾ in) long
- Strong elastic bands

Tools:

- Wallpaper scraper
- Sharp scalpel or blade
- Scissors
- Bradawl or sharp, pointed tool to make a hole
- Needle and thread

Silver birch bark is the most exciting and rewarding material to work with. Museums are rich in examples of how birch bark has been used by cultures around the world, particularly by Native Americans, to make canoes, shoes, cradles and vessels of all kinds, as well as for medicine. There are also strong historical traditions of using birch bark in Northern Scandinavia and Russia, countries thickly forested with birch, for boxes, hats and basket weaving. It is a beautiful and much-loved tree, valued by cultures around the world for its many and varied uses, and lauded in folksongs and ballads. Today however, with such a wide range of materials available for designers and artists to use, bark is less popular despite its strength, flexibility and longevity.

Following in the footsteps of our forefathers, we will make a silver birch bark vessel, using a glass jam jar or tin can for the inner container. This can be used as a lantern with a tea-light inside and would be ideal as outdoor lighting, perfect for a summer barbeque! Make sure the jar or can you are using is big enough to completely contain the tea-light, keeping it well away from the bark, which is highly flammable. Do not use any candle larger than a tea-light and never leave the light unattended, even when outside.

COLLECTING AND MAKING

Bark is the protective outer coating of the tree. It grows with the tree and takes its character from the environmental conditions. Silver birch bark, which we are using here, ranges from paper thin to a leathery texture, depending on the type of birch tree and the conditions it grew in.

Birch bark must only be collected from a tree that has already been felled by the landowner or has fallen naturally. Taking bark from a live tree will cause lasting damage or even kill the tree, so make sure you choose a dead or fallen tree. Make sure you always have permission from the landowner before you remove any bark and never take from a conservation area.

When you find a fallen tree or log, the wood inside will be rotting away, leaving the bark almost completely intact. The bark is full of resinous oils so it will not decay. If the bark still feels firmly attached to the tree then it will be pointless to attempt to remove it. Make a note of where it is and come back in a few months to check if it has loosened. If the bark feels loose and slightly saggy on the tree then it is ready to remove.

Opposite *You can light the tea-light or use a battery operated tea-light for a warm glow.*

Above Sections of bark like this will often be stripped by wild animals, such as badgers and deer, looking for food.

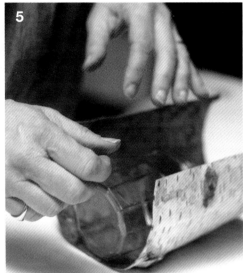

1 Wear old clothes for collecting bark. You will be kneeling in the ground and the bark will be dirty, especially on the inside. Look out for small animals like toads and insects, which live inside the bark and may be difficult to spot. Try not to disturb them if possible, and choose a different tree if necessary.

Decide which area of bark you are removing. It should be a smooth and unblemished section if possible. Gently bash the trunk all round with a blunt tool, as this will help loosen the bark and make it easier to remove.

2 Slice with a sharp blade in a line along the bark and ease it open very carefully.

3 Using the scraper, loosen the bark and start to peel it back. Try to keep the bark in one piece. If it breaks up, don't worry, you can adapt the project accordingly.

4 At home, clean inside the bark with a scraper and scrub it with wire wool and water. I use a bucket of water outside for this, to save blocking up the sink! If the bark is fragile or thin, you will need to be gentle, laying it down flat and scraping in one direction only, to avoid tearing. If it is a tougher piece of bark it may take several hours to clean. I leave tough bits of wood and dirt on the inside of the bark if they are difficult to remove. They can add character and even strength to the work!

If the bark is soft enough to work, then it can be used straight away, treating it as if it were cardboard or thin leather. If it is rather dry or hard, then soak in a sink full of very hot water for up to an hour, or hold carefully over steam from the kettle. Steaming it this way will soften it surprisingly quickly in just a few minutes.

5 Choose a container with straight sides to fit the height of the bark. If using a tin can, you may want to rust it for a more subtle effect. Do this by spraying with salt water regularly and leaving outside in the rain for several weeks. Cut a piece of bark to fit your container. Wrap the bark tightly around the sides of the container and secure temporarily with several strong elastic bands. Slide the bark off the container. You now know exactly how wide to make it.

6 Pierce through the bark with a strong needle or bradawl to prepare 2 sets of 2 holes to sew through. If the bark is thin or soft enough, you can just use the needle directly.

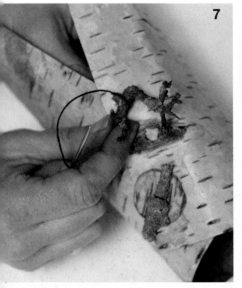

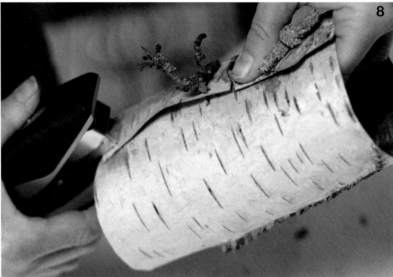

7 Cut a 20 cm (8 in) length of waxed thread. Thread it from the inside, through one hole, round the toggle several times, and back through the second hole. Tie a knot on the inside – it is very fiddly working from inside the container, but persevere – it can be done and will look much neater with the knot hidden inside. Repeat for the second hole with a different toggle. The bark sleeve will now fit neatly over the top of the container.

8 I don't think it's cheating too much to use a strong stapler and put in a few staples to keep the shape and make it neater. The staples can be perfectly disguised as lenticels, or pores, in the bark and will hardly be noticed.

Try to keep the staples at the same angle as the natural lenticels and they will blend in even better. You can also paint over the staples very carefully with black metal paint if you wish.

IDEAS FOR EXTRA TIME

Silver birch bark has different-sized dark lines or lenticels on the surface, which are pores to allow gases to pass through. With the scalpel, gently clean inside each one by pushing the dirt out. This will allow the light to shine through more brightly.

A simpler, and very quick, alternative for this project is to use smaller pieces of bark that are often left on the woodland floor by wild animals. Wrap these pieces of bark round the chosen container, overlapping them as you go, with the rough edges on view for a more rustic result. Make sure the bark doesn't overlap the container at the top or it will become a fire hazard.

Secure with several elastic bands, just to hold in place, whilst you tie waxed thread or even vines and ivy branches as tightly as possible around the container. Remove elastic bands for the final result.

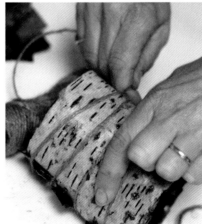

Right The bark vase sets off the beautiful colours of the dried chillis.

Feather wreath

Feathers may seem an unusual material to use for a wreath, but in fact will give you a very long-lasting, sturdy Christmas decoration, for indoors or outside, and will make a bold impact on any wall.

Feathers are so often thrown away, yet they are extraordinary, complex and very beautiful objects. They are designed for flight, protection, warmth, decoration and waterproofing and have been celebrated and valued greatly in cultures throughout the world. Often colourful, they have been considered a mark of wealth, status and spirituality throughout history.

Materials:

- Approximately 70 bird feathers of any kind: pigeon, pheasant, turkey, duck will all be fine
- 150 cm (59 in) length of vine/ soft branch
- 24 sticks of florist wire (each approx. 20 cm/8 in)
- Roll of Jute twine
- Reel of florist's wire

Tools:

- Scissors
- Wire cutters
- Secateurs

Note:

- You can always create a basic circular form from thick wire if you are unable to find the vine materials naturally. (Curl the wire round two or three times to a diameter of 40 cm (15¾ in) and then wrap the wire around again to strengthen it.)

COLLECTING AND MAKING

This wreath is made of bronze turkey feathers because a kind friend, who keeps a few heritage birds for Christmas, handed them over, if somewhat quizzically! The colours are beautiful compared to the more common breeds. Small-scale turkey farmers will be very pleased to hand over the feathers, particularly if you order a turkey at the same time. Ask a month before Christmas, or again near Easter when birds are plucked ready for the market.

You could just as easily use grey/white pigeon feathers, which can be found almost everywhere, in town and country, but are often unfairly considered slightly 'dirty', or more pleasant waterfowl and duck feathers, which can be found by canals and lakes in abundance. For the less squeamish, in the UK you can find plenty of pheasants as road kill towards winter: the feathers will pull out easily and make a magnificent display. Take the bird home and use rubber gloves as a caution.

Feathers can also be purchased in fly fishing shops, online (beware of being sold protected bird feathers) or ask at a bird sanctuary, farm or a local gardener, who keep doves or ducks. They may be very pleased to have you come along and clean up after the birds, which lose their feathers regularly throughout the year. There is no one moulting season for wild birds; feathers are lost gradually throughout the year.

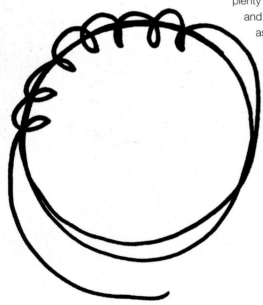

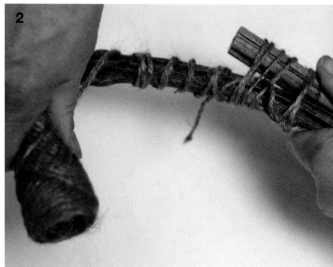

1 To keep the wreath as natural as possible, I used a length of wild clematis vine, 150 cm (59 in) long, found in the hedgerow. It was soft enough to curl into a large circle, with a diameter of 40 cm (15¾ in). You can also use other trailing vines such as fresh soft ivy branches, grapevine or wisteria, but not dried materials, as they will be too brittle to bend. This will form the base of the wreath but will be hidden by the feathers.

Select a section of vine that will bend round easily. It doesn't need to be an exact circle. If you can't find good vine, see the note on p.48 for an alternative.

2 Cut your length of vine, bend it round, and weave into a roughly circular shape. Tie the end of the jute twine to the top of the wreath and wind it tightly all around the circle. Finally use the end to make a little loop for hanging the wreath up when you have finished.

3 Now to the feathers. It will be easier to work on a tabletop for this part. Wash the hollow shaft ends of the feathers in warm soapy water and lay them out across the table. Group them into mixed bundles of five feathers each and bind them tightly at the base with a piece of florist wire. Feathers are very tough, so be firm and bind each bundle as tightly as possible. Make up 12 of these bundles, ready to use. You can make a few more if needed later.

4 First, wrap the reel wire around your starting point on the wreath. Holding the wreath in your left hand, position the first bundle of feathers. Bind the bundle tightly, four or five times, onto the wreath with the wire.

5 Move onto the second bunch and bind it on to cover the wire of the previous bundle. Continue in this way all round the circle.

6 When you have completed the circle, you can tweak and pull the feathers into the best position.
   If there are any gaps or thinner places, push a new feather under the wire to add to it. A shorter feather will result in a more 'chunky' wreath, whereas a longer feather, such as from a pheasant, will be wider overall.

7 When you are happy with the shape of the wreath, you can hang it on your door, inside or out, as a festive decoration that will last many years (see the photo on p.49).

You could add other material to the feather
bundles, as long as they are firm. The reddish
stems from horse chestnut tree leaves and
Virginia creeper will add colour and contrast.

You could make the wreath from bunches of
lavender, conifer branches, mixed green foliage
from the hedgerow, or bundles of leaves.

This page Caroline
Sharp, Leaf Circle, 2004.
Bay leaves and willow,
40 x 60 cm (16 x 24 in).
Photo: Caroline Sharp.

Silver birch bark brooch

This is a highly unusual piece of jewellery which, without fail, attracts attention and interest. People are always surprised that this feather-shaped brooch comes from the bark of a tree and are fascinated by the colour, texture and patterns in the bark. To some, it suggests a feather, to others a leaf or even a mountain range. It certainly reminds us that similar shapes and patterns recur throughout the natural world. The bark is lightweight, waterproof, soft but strong, and perfect for its use as a brooch.

Materials:
- Section of silver birch bark with scar shape
- Metal brooch backing or recycled pin brooch

Tools:
- PVA glue or super glue
- Sandpaper
- Sharp scissors or knife

Left The finished brooch will look amazing against a colourful scarf or jacket.

COLLECTING AND MAKING

For full instructions on collecting the bark, see p. 45 in the tea-light holder project.

When you gather bark in the woodlands, you will notice a recurring mark like a gash or scar in the bark, where a branch has grown off the main trunk. These are very common and when you find a supply of silver birch bark in the woods, there will be a number of such shapes if you hunt for them.

1 The bark will not dry out or change significantly, so you can get started on this project straight away. Using large kitchen scissors, cut around the 'gash' as widely as possible, in a leaf shape. There will be the inevitable obstructions and holes in the bark, which will dictate the overall shape. Don't worry if it looks one-sided. Bark is a natural material and each piece will always be different.

Strong kitchen scissors will cut through the bark easily. Scrape away any residue wood inside the piece of bark and clean with a scraper or wire wool. Don't worry about cleaning all the dirt off, as long as it is not loose or messy. It will help strengthen the brooch! (See p.45 for image of scraping.)

2 Using sandpaper work around the edge of the leaf shape to add a bevelled edge all round.

3 You can also add a pattern by scraping into the 'leaf' and making marks with a tool such as a blade or chisel. Apply a little wax all over the front and sides of the bark and polish it well, using a cloth to further bring out the texture and colour of the bark.

4 Using PVA or super glue, attach a pin brooch backing to the back of the brooch, at the top and in the flattest place. Leave overnight to dry.

5 Jewellery fixings can be purchased from craft shops or department stores. You could also recycle an existing pin badge (as shown in the photo) that you no longer want and glue that to the back of the leaf.

IDEAS FOR EXTRA TIME

If you glue a small magnet onto the reverse, these leaves also look good on the fridge! Magnets can be bought on the internet (try Amazon), or you can use a self-adhesive magnet purchased from a good craft shop.

Stick mobile

Materials:
- Waxed linen thread
- Sticks of dogwood, or other straight sticks, approx. 12 cm (4¾ in) long

Tools:
- Scissors
- Secateurs

- -

If you find smaller pieces from nature that you particularly like, one easy but effective way to preserve and enjoy them is to string them together in a mobile, to hang from the ceiling, window or in the garden.

My favourite items to use are sticks of dogwood, which grow in long, straight lengths and retain their colour after cutting, looking impressive against a white background. It is a common, hardy shrub grown in gardens and parks, particularly in heavy clay soils. Gardeners cut it back hard in early spring, so you may be able to get it ready-cut if you ask.

The colour will change a little over time as the sticks dry out but the artwork will last many years.

- -

Right The mobile will not last as long outside (especially with an inquisitive cat living nearby) but it looks interesting as it weathers and changes colour.

This longer mobile, made to hang outside in the garden, took 4 hours to make but became a relaxing project to pick up in the evenings. It also makes a pleasant tinkling sound as it moves in the breeze.

When hanging up, the sticks will move around and jut out at different angles, creating interesting patterns. If hung indoors, you can train a spotlight on it and make some impressive shadows for added effect.

Left Red dogwood (Cornus sanguinea), 2012. Photo: Jane Bevan.

COLLECTING AND MAKING

1 Strip off any leaves and select straight lengths to cut from. Cut the lengths of dogwood into 12 cm (4½ in) sticks with secateurs but don't use the very thin top ends.

If the stick is bent then gently straighten it out by shaping it over your leg when you are sitting down.

2 Cut a long length of black waxed linen thread, double it over, and tie a full knot around the middle of the first stick. The sticks will shrivel a little over time as they dry out, so a tight knot will help.

3 Keep tying more sticks as tightly as possible. Be aware, though, that waxed thread knots are very hard to undo, so be sure it is in the right place first. If one knot is too loose, then the stick will fall out and it is difficult to mend.

4 You can stop at any time when you are happy with the length. If you have a plan for hanging it, perhaps in the window, the corner of a room or outside, you can measure up and make it fit exactly.

If you run out of thread just tie the old piece off and double up a new piece of thread. Tie that onto the last stick, as well as the previous piece of string, so it cannot slide off. When you reach the end of your mobile, trim the sticks all to the same length to tidy it up.

5 Finally, take two slightly larger sticks and tie them across each other. Use the spare ends of the thread to make a hanging loop.

6 Tie this onto the mobile and then hang it from a hook or nail in the ceiling, from a beam or in a window.

5

IDEAS FOR EXTRA TIME

Try tying together a mixture of natural materials – twigs, feathers, stones, leaves and seeds, perhaps all from one day out.

Try cutting tiny sections of tendrils from wild clematis (clematis vitalba or 'Old Man's Beard') in winter, an invasive tangled plant that grows naturally in hedgerows and has wonderful, coiled, spring-like tendrils. Tie them in the same way as the dogwood for a very unusual display.

6

Pine needle coiled basket

Natural materials such as rushes, willow and grasses are perfect for basket-making and have been used for centuries around the world. Techniques include stake and strand, plaiting, weaving and assembly, but one of the easiest and most satisfying techniques is coiling. Here we will make two small, contrasting coiled baskets – one using pine needles and one using horse hair.

Materials:

- Fresh or dried pine needles 10 cm (4 in) long, at least a plastic carrier bag full

Tools:

- Large-eye needle
- Trimits waxed thread, 22 metres (72 feet), black or white for different effects. Or beeswax holder as alternative option (if preferred) and thick linen thread
- Scissors

Above A small Tit's nest which uses horse hair in the lining. The structure of the nest is very similar to that of a basket and the nest serves a similar function of storage and protection.

Top right Detail of pine needles coiled together.

Right A small horse hair basket, see p. 65.

Far right Finished pine neeedle basket, Jane Bevan.

COLLECTING AND MAKING

Pine trees have a great many wonderful, life-affirming properties and can be used in a number of practical ways. The needles are rich in iron and vitamins A and C. They can help hunger and tiredness, strengthen the heart and act as anti-oxidants if chewed raw or made into tea. I don't necessarily recommend this, but it is something joyful and wholesome to consider when you contemplate your finished basket!

The great thing about pine needles, apart from their lovely long-lasting smell, is that they are evergreen and can be found at any time of the year worldwide. There are over 100 species of pine trees in forests, gardens and parks, and most have needles that can be used, providing they are at least 10 cm (4 in) in length. The green colour will fade but that is part of the joy of the materials – watching them gradually change over time. Collect pine needles from the ground and use them green and fresh or when they are dried and faded, either will work fine (if dried, soak them for 24 hours in warm water to soften first). This project can be done in one go or you can take more time over it and do a little every day. Seeing the basket grow and take shape can be very satisfying.

GLYCERINE BATH TIP

Over time, the pine needles will shrivel and the basket may become loose. This can be prevented by soaking it in a glycerine bath when you are finished. Artist Anna King uses this technique for her baskets, she says: 'Dilute the glycerine with water in a ratio of 1:2; immerse the basket, ensuring it is covered and leave for 48 hours, turning it occasionally. Take it out, drain it and allow to dry naturally in an airy, dry place for at least two days.'

1 Wash the pine needles well in warm, soapy water. Each pine needle has a 'woody' butt at the end, which you can leave in place, as I have done, or scrape off using your thumbnail or a sharp knife for a smoother look.

2 Gather the needles together into small bundles of 14 to 16 needles, or a total diameter of 1 cm (½ in). Tie a single knot tightly around the middle of the bunch, using waxed thread to make it easier to work.

3 You will need approximately 22 metres (72 feet) or 1 packet Trimits waxed thread. It can be expensive, so consider making your own instead; buy a beeswax holder from a craft store and pull any strong thread several times slowly through the wax.

Wrap the thread round into a ball shape to make it easier to use. In addition, don't waste any little bits of cut-off waxed thread. They will come in useful at other times.

There are several ways to start a coiled basket, but I suggest tying the waxed thread, already threaded onto a needle, tightly around the first bundle 2½ cm (1 in) from the butt end. Then wind the thread around the bundle, down as far as the butt.

Holding it tight, bend the bundle back on itself and stitch through both sides to attach together.

4 Then start to wind the bundle round in a circle and sew it into place evenly as you go, sewing from back to front. I have used simple, long running stitches so that you can still clearly see the pine needles underneath.

5 Pull the thread as tightly as you can to keep the shape of the basket and make it stronger.

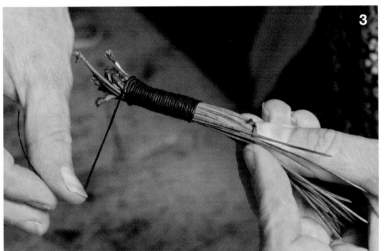

6a & 6b When you need to add a new bundle of pine needles, just force the ends in and sew over the join. Check on both sides of the coiling that the thread goes all around the pine needles, trapping them in to the stitching. If a few pine needles protrude, don't worry, as they will get caught up in the basket as you go along.

7 If you run out of thread, just tie in a new length and tuck the knot inside the pine needles to hide it. The stitches will become wider apart as the coiled base grows, but try to keep the stitches in a line if you want a neater look.

8 Continue coiling a flat circle until you are happy with the size. This will now be the base.

9 When you are ready to begin the sides of the basket, start to position the new bundles at an angle on top of the bundle beneath, and stitch in place. You can have a steady rise to the basket, or more vertical sides depending on how you angle the bundles. Experiment with the size and shape of the basket until you are ready to finish. After the final bundle has been sewn in place, tie off the thread in a knot and tuck it out of sight into the pine needles.

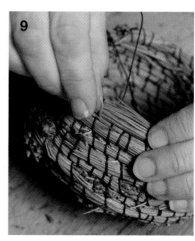

Horse hair is a strong and highly versatile material, traditionally used to make brushes, upholstery, musical instrument string, fishing line and even jewellery.

It can be used to make a coiled basket although it will be a challenge to get hold of supplies, so gather the hair whenever you see it. It might be from the fields where horses live or have been clipped outside, or ask a local horse owner or at an equestrian centre. It is also available on the internet through a number of companies, but can be very expensive.

Horse hair from the mane and the tail can be used. It has a very waxy texture and handling it takes a little getting used to. Wash well first in warm, soapy water, then gather the strands of hair into small bundles. Try to use hair that is approximately 10 cm (4 in) long or more, otherwise it will be too fiddly. Make up around 20 of these bundles before you start on the basket.

Continue coiling the bundles of horse hair in the same way as the pine needles, stitching as evenly and tightly as possible. Some of the hairs will be sticking out, so you can trim it with scissors to tidy it up or leave as it is and keep the slightly 'wild' look.

Above *Due to the small amount of horse hair you will have, the basket will be precious and small in size.*

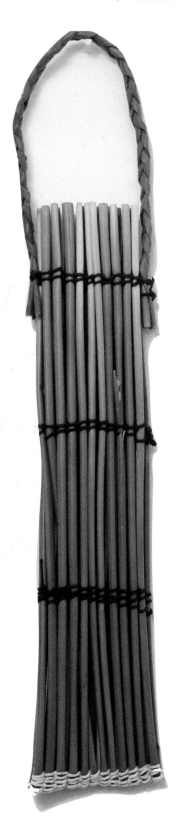

Twined decorative baskets

Reeds – tall grass-like plants – are fairly common in wet, marshy areas and are wonderful materials to work with. They are strong, pliable, glossy and a deep, beautiful shade of green. The different species have been used over the years in a great many ways, including for thatching, basket-making and furniture-making. As an alternative, you could use rushes, grasses, straw and birch bark, or any materials that are supple enough to bend and twist but not break.

These baskets are small (limited by the length of the reeds I have used) and although not functional, they do look stunning as a set of three pinned up on the wall. When the colours eventually fade, they will develop a rich straw colour that is just as appealing. They are at their best from spring onwards, but it is possible to pop a bunch into your freezer for use later in the year too!

Don't worry about being too exact with this project. It doesn't need to be perfect and, as always, any mistakes may well add to the overall look of the work. See p. 23 for further information on the twining technique.

- -

Materials:
- 15 small, thin reeds, each at least 40 cm (15¾ in) long
- 1 packet Trimits waxed thread, approx. 20 m (66 ft) long
- 6–8 pine needles for decoration

Tools:
- Scissors
- Pencil

- -

COLLECTING AND MAKING

1 The first step Is to select around 10 strong reeds, all a similar length (although they can vary in thickness). The ones used here are 40 cm (15¾ in) long when picked. When collecting, try to get right to the base of each reed as you cut it, because you will get a much longer length to work with.

Remove any leaves or rough, loose material and lay them flat together on the table. Always have a few spare to hand as some may get damaged as you go along.

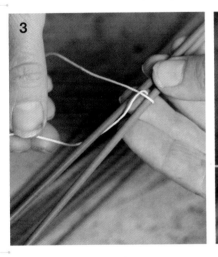

2 You will need a lot of waxed thread, but start by cutting one metre, as that is easy to work with. Change your thread; white thread will have good contrast, whereas brown and black will be less noticeable. Double the thread over and, starting with the reed on the far left, wrap it round approximately in the middle of the reed.

3 Now take the half that is nearest to you, around the back of the second reed, and tug gently into place. Keep going in a consistent pattern, twining the reeds together. This is fiddly but once all the reeds are attached it will hold together much better.

Take your time and pull gently after each move to keep it as neat and regular as possible.

IDEAS FOR EXTRA TIME

As an extra feature, you can add pine needles, small feathers or seed pods by tucking them into the twining at the top of the basket.

4 At the end of the first line, turn the reeds over and continue again from the left until you have completed around five lines or used up the thread. Tie a small knot to secure the reeds, and this now forms the base.

5 Using a pencil to hold them in place, gently bend the reeds up from the base on each side (now called the uprights) and trim reeds to the same length all round.

6 Now you can choose whether to twine with more waxed thread or with more reeds to continue the basket, leaving gaps for effect. If you use more reeds for twining, try to choose long, thin ones, which bend more easily than those with thicker, more woody bases. Experiment with colours and patterns to give each basket its own character. I rarely plan or design the pattern in advance, but just see how the materials guide me.

7 Bend your chosen reed or thread in half and again wrap round the far left reed to start. Then continue twining. You will need to concentrate on consistent twining and be sure not to leave out an upright.

If the reed/thread breaks or runs out, just tuck the ends inside the basket out of sight. Then prepare a new length, bend it double and begin again in the same place. When you have reached the top of the basket, and are happy with the pattern, trim the ends of the reeds across in a straight line.

8 Finally, make a handle by plaiting together three lengths of reed. Tie the three reeds together at the top, bring the far left to the middle, then the far right to the middle and repeat until you reach the end.

9 Handles can then be tied onto the sides of the basket with a small piece of thread, or woven into the top of the basket by inserting them into the twining as you go.

Below These three baskets have now faded to a more subtle colour.

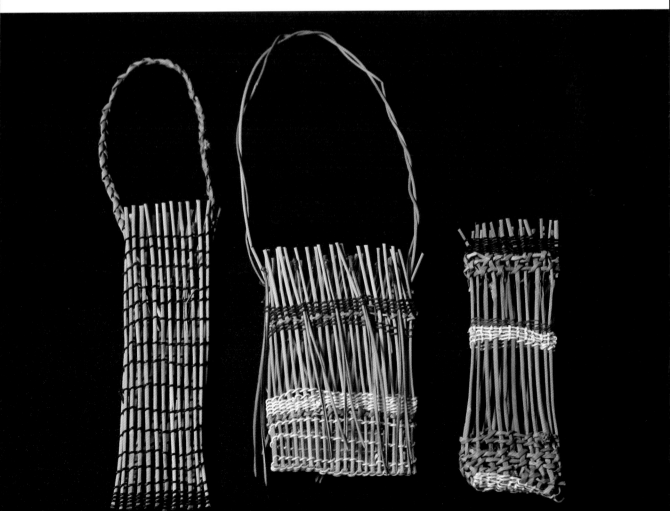

Besom-style broom

A besom broom is a simple but effective broom made over many centuries for brushing and sweeping. They were traditionally made using heather, furze or twigs, usually birch, tied around a pole to form a rounded broom. They are very popular today and there are still specialist professional craftspeople who continue this rare craft.

However with a little practise and determination you can make a serviceable besom-style broom yourself. They are amazingly robust and efficient, especially at clearing leaves off the lawn, and they have lots of character too – no two are alike!

It is impossible to avoid the connection to witches brooms so bear that in mind too… a young fan of the 'magic arts' will be very pleased with a broom like this at Halloween time. So much nicer than buying from a shop!

Materials:
- Birch twigs to make a bundle 60 cm (2 ft) in length and 28 cm (11 in) in diameter
- Long pole or straight stick in any strong wood, 1.2 m (4 ft) in length and 10 cm (4 in) in diameter
- Split cane, or similar, purchased from craft shop and soaked overnight

Tools:
- Long plastic cable ties or string
- Scissors
- Secateurs
- Small, short-handled axe
- Wood saw

Note:
- All measurements are approximate depending on what materials you find and how you want the final product to look.

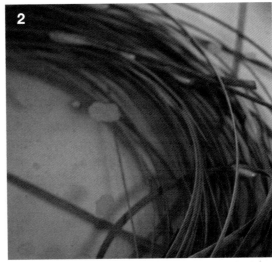

COLLECTING AND MAKING

1 Search for some suitable soft twigs in a garden or countryside, birch twigs are ideal. I found these when a friend was clearing the garden, you will find that people are always happy for you to take away their garden rubbish! They had been cut down some time previously so were dried out already but if you use freshly cut material you will need to leave them in a dry location for a few weeks first. Otherwise they may shrivel over time and the broom will become loose.

2 Meanwhile soak a bundle of split canes, purchased from a craft shop, in water overnight to soften ready to use for the binding.

3 Gather together the twigs into a bundle around 60 cm (2 ft) in length and 28 cm (11 in) in diameter. The twigs will be fiddly to handle so be firm and treat them with a strong grip.

4a & 4b To secure the bundle temporarily, wrap plastic cable ties or string around them as tightly as possible.

5

6

5 Now that you have the bundle under tight control, tie the soft and soaked split cane tightly around the bundles 4 or 5 times and tuck the end neatly inside the binding. Cut away the cable ties or string as their job is done and the bundle will now stay in shape.

6 Select the stick or handle you plan to use and use a saw to cut it to around 1.2 m (4 ft) in length.

Find a strong bench or surface to work on and keep hands clear of the saw.

7a & 7b Using a short-handled axe, take a few minutes to shape the end of the stick (not the handle end) into a point. Always wear good tough boots when working with sharp tools, ideally steel-capped boots if you have them, and be very careful of hands and feet. Store the axe away safely after use.

A sharp axe is much safer than a blunt one so keep your tools in good condition. A local hardware or tool shop will be able to sharpen tools for you.

To further secure the broom a wooden dowel or peg was traditionally inserted through the bundle and into a hole, drilled first in the handle. This would stop the broom coming apart over time. My broom is for lighter duties so I won't need to this time.

7a

7b

8 Ram the sharp end of the pole into the middle of the bundle by banging down onto the ground gradually or forcing it in. Check it is going into the centre as it is difficult to pull out and start again.

The pole should be hidden from view and the broom will be surprisingly tight and sturdy. Use the secateurs to tidy the top of the bundle. Keep the broom in a dry place and it should last a good few years.

8

Walking sticks and canes

To make a top-quality walking stick (with a lifetime of use ahead of it), is a highly skilled art, perfected over many years by traditional, independent craftspeople. Nothing however beats the satisfaction and fun of making one yourself and in just a couple of days you too can make a simple but perfectly useable stick of your own, by taking advantage of the natural shape of the stick. You can search for sticks in woodlands (with permission from the landowner) or find them in friends' and neighbours' gardens, particularly if there has been a garden clearance. Do not take anything from a living tree; it will be easy to find a few sticks lying on the ground, especially after a storm or high winds. The more you look, the more interesting shapes you will see and it's a great project for all the family on a walk. Children love to use walking sticks too, especially if they had a hand in the selection of the stick.

Sticks can be made of ash, hazel, cherry, beech and other more unusual woods, or even driftwood, as long as the sticks are light, straight and strong enough. They can be plain and functional or highly decorative, with ornate handles (usually bone, horn or wood) or even with compasses and whistles built in. Wood carries a warmth and natural beauty that makes it a pleasure to make and use, providing a close and sustainable connection with the woodlands and countryside.

Sticks range from straightforward walking sticks, wading staffs for fishing and hiking sticks to elegant, decorative canes. Not just for the elderly, sticks are widely used by walkers: to lessen the impact on joints, to help with going up and down hills, or to simply lean on while admiring the view!

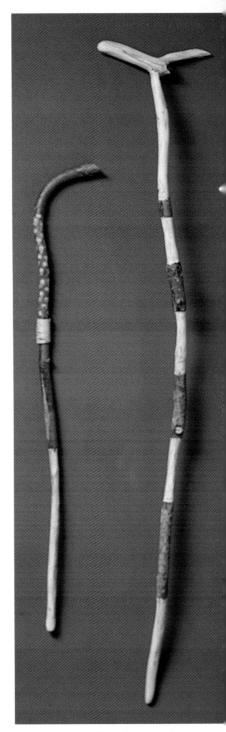

Above Canes can be mounted on the wall, displayed in an umbrella stand or given as an unusual gift.

Materials:
- Rubber tips or ferrules
- Sandpaper – smooth and coarse
- Small selection of sticks ranging from 1.2 to 1.5 metres (4–6 ft) in length and 8 cm (3 in) in diameter
- Wax, linseed or teak oil
- Wood glue or PVA

- Protective eye wear
- Protective gloves
- Small pocket saw

Note:
- All measurements are approximate depending on what materials you find and how you want the final product to look.

Tools:
- Face mask
- Penknife

COLLECTING AND MAKING

1 Take a small saw out with you and cut sticks into the basic shape on-site to save hauling home a longer branch than you will need.

Take extra care if you are alone in the woods and take a mobile phone and mini first aid kit with you. It is so easy to get carried away searching for sticks and forget about safety. Cut away from you and always put the blade carefully away after each use. Never walk around with the blade out and look out for eye hazards too.

2 Select a few sticks – you are looking for a length of around 1.5 metres or 5–6 feet, and width around 8 cm or 3 inches in diameter. Also a pleasing shape, unusual characteristics (maybe a twist in the stick or unusual bark) and strength.

Test the strength by carefully pushing down hard to see if it snaps or smash the stick against a rock. Many sticks may break before you find the right one but it is worth being choosy for all the work you will be putting in.

Above Sticks ready for testing.

The stick needs to be relatively straight with the top directly above the base. Professional walking stick makers may straighten the stick or shank first using heat treatment but you can also use a kink or twist part way along to add to the character. If you are looking for a stick that really lasts generations then you need to dry the wood out slowly for as long as a year or until it is fully seasoned. Seasoned wood has the moisture adequately reduced so the wood is stronger, lighter, easier to work, less prone to cracking and less attractive to insects and fungus.

To season wood, stack it above the ground with the air circulating around the sticks in a dry, well-ventilated place. Do not put the wood near

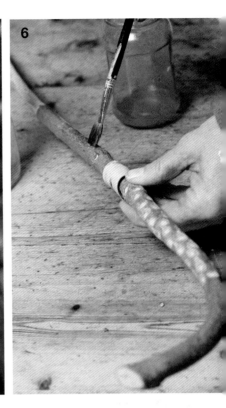

radiators or hot surfaces as the drying will be too fast and it will crack quite quickly. You can of course skip this stage if you wish and just select a dry, healthy looking stick and hope for the best!

3 Remove any small branches with a saw working down the length of the stick. Wearing protective gloves is recommended.

4 Remove any bark by peeling it away with hands or scraping it off with a sharp knife. Always cut away from your body and be aware at all times where your hands and fingers are in relation to the blade. Leave for about a week in a dry place if the wood still feels damp.

5 Wrap sandpaper round a block of wood and sand the stick whilst wearing a small face mask and eye protection. Do not inhale the dust and try to work outside if possible. Start with a coarse sandpaper and finish with a smoother paper to get a really good finish.

Sand down particularly hard on any rough areas or knots in the wood.

6 The shank can be varnished or treated with linseed, teak oil or beeswax for protection from the weather and for a richer surface finish. Spread it on with a cloth or brush and wipe off any excess before leaving to dry.

THUMB STICK IDEA

A popular version is the 'thumb stick' which can easily be cut to shape and can be gripped comfortably.

7a

7b

Below *When searching for sticks, you will come across many that are not strong enough to be used for walking (as discussed in step 2). If they are appealing then use them anyway to make decorative canes, reminiscent of those used by fashionable gentlemen over the last centuries. Taking time carving into the stick can be a very relaxing and absorbing occupation so find a lovely spot to sit in and enjoy the experience.*

7a & 7b A further simple, decorative effect can be achieved by gouging out a shallow hole in the wooden handle with a sharp tool to make room for a shallow stone or pebble. Glue the stone into place (using any strong glue) and leave to dry.

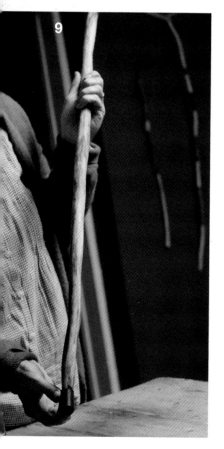

9

8 Finally a rubber or metal tip or ferrule will aid stability for the user and protect the end from the hard ground. These can be bought online (for example through Amazon) or in hardware stores. Buy a selection of sizes (they only cost pennies), find one which fits well and glue it in place.

TIP

If you want to cut a few corners but still want to make your own stick then take a look at online websites where you can sign up to a stick-making course, buy a DIY kit or a wide range of seasoned 'shanks' or sticks ready to use with all the accessories. Try www.thestickman. co.uk in North Yorkshire.

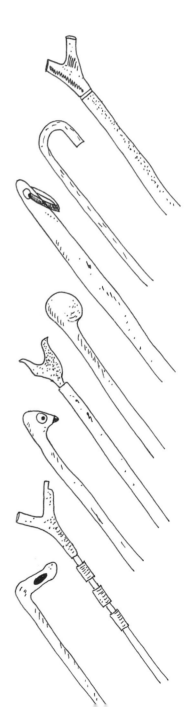

Left *My neighbour Geoff Holt has been making walking sticks in his workshop for 40 years. He harvests the sticks in winter and dries them out, often over several years, ready for use later on.*

Below *Walking sticks made by local craftsmen in India, formed from branches and roots, 2006. Private collection of Helen Juffs and Deirdre Figueiredo.*

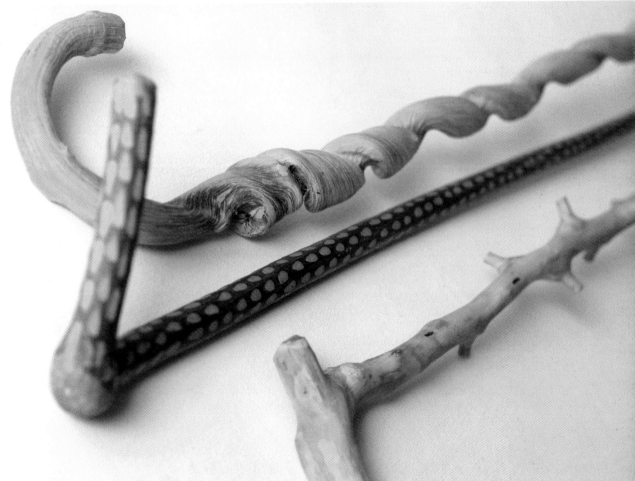

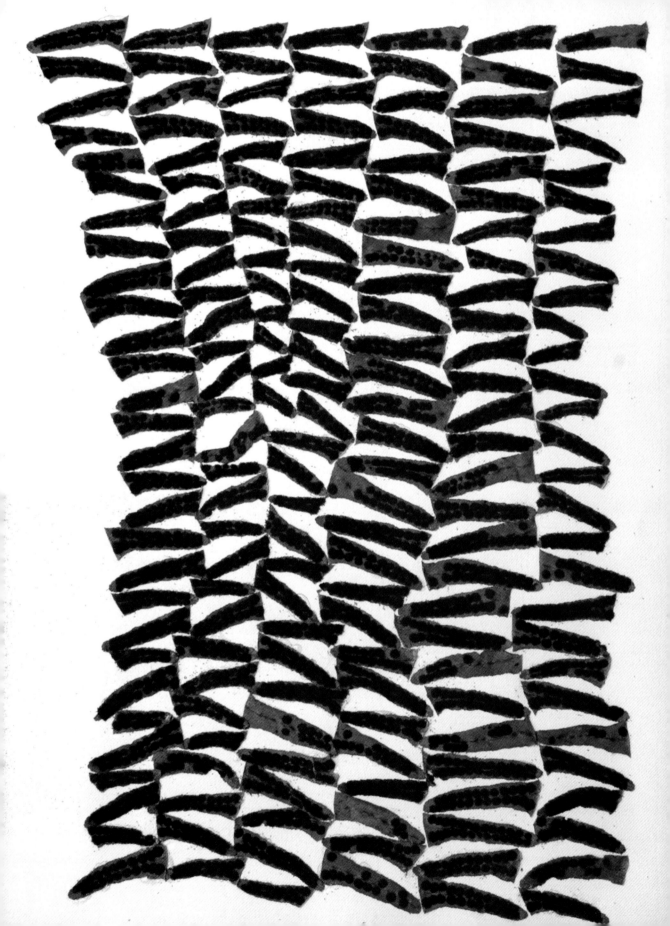

Gallery

Page 78: Marian Bijlenga, Written Weed, 2004. Fern collage number 101, 42 x 31 cm (16½ x 12 in). From a limited edition book, each collage is made from natural materials and is meticulously arranged, acting as a moment of contemplation and a reminder of the place. Photo: Marian Bijlenga.

Page 79, right: Sarah Hood, Malden Avenue East Necklace (from Structural Series #1: Decomposition), 1999. Sterling silver, Chinese lantern pods, 20 x 20 x 3 cm (8 x 8 x 1 in). In the collection of Tacoma Art Museum. Photo: Doug Yaple.

Opposite: Kate Gilliland, Sleeping Mouse, 2009. Silver, found mouse, 2.5 x 6 x 5 cm (1 x 2½ x 2 in). Kate creates intriguing, fantastical jewellery and objects using found animal remains. She found this little mouse in her boyfriend's bathroom. She freeze-dried the mouse to preserve it and made the little leather pillow and silver case to keep it safe. Photo: Chris Webb.

Below: Jane Bevan, selection of bark vessels, 2012. Silver birch bark sewn with waxed thread, average size 20 x 10 cm (8 x 4 in). Photo: Paul Tupman.

Left: Susie Vaughan, Blackberry Picker, *2007. This basket is woven with a variety of colourful natural materials found growing in hedgerows and gardens, including ash, red dogwood, Australian bottlebrush and willow, including salix daphnoides irrorata, 23 x 40 cm (9 x 16 in). Photo: Susie Vaughan.*

Below: Anna King, Lippy, *(detail) 2010. Coiled basket form, pine needles, waxed linen, peacock feathers, book with poem, 16 x 11 cm (6 x 4½ in). Photo: A.S. King.*

Right: Stella Harding, Burr (Natural Velcro), *2011. Burdock seed heads, 20 x 12 cm (7¾ x 4¾ in). 'I made the first version of Burr after spotting some dried burdock seed-heads in a local park. I remembered how, as kids, we used to throw them at each other, delighting in the way the hundreds of tiny barbs stuck tenaciously to our clothes. I took them straight to the studio and in minutes, using only the natural 'velcro-like' properties of the seed-heads, had assembled a surprisingly robust basket. My fingers tingled for hours afterwards, though!' Photo: Trevor Springett.*

Left: Lizzie Farey, Nest Form, *2011. Dimensions: 10 x 21 cm (4 x 8¼ in). Photo: Shannon Tofts.*

Right: Dail Behennah, Pebble Dish, *2002. White willow, silver-plated pins, stainless steel wire, pebbles, 56 x 56 x 5 cm (22 x 22 x 2 in). Photo: Jason Ingram.*

Left: Kirsty Elson, Church Row, *2012. Old piece of deckchair with stripy canvas attached and drift-wood, 50 x 10 cm (20 x 4 in). 'I am totally led by the materials I find: I get ridiculously excited every time I find an interesting piece of driftwood on the beach!' Photo: Kirsty Elson.*

Right: Stephen Butler, Arcane Specimen Vol.3i, *2005. Mixed media assemblage, 7.9 x 19.7 x 12.3 cm (3 x 8 x 5 in). Photo: Stephen Butler.*

Conclusion: what next?

If you have begun hunting for materials and tried a number of the projects in this book, I hope you will be seeing the natural world around you, in all its wonderful detail, with fresh eyes. Wondering where do you go from here? These are a few suggestions to try:

- Be proud of what you have made and look after it – it is totally unique and your own lovely work!

- Display it in your home for others to enjoy and admire. You could get together with other artists and organise a small exhibition at the local library, festival or community centre. If there are empty shop windows nearby, you can sometimes get permission to set up a display free of charge. You could enter into a local art exhibition, or an open exhibition at an art gallery. Displaying your work is a great way to get feedback from others.

- Look for a local art group you could join. It will keep you making and is a great way to share ideas, knowledge and enthusiasm.

- Keep looking for new materials when you are out and about. They will give you inspiration to make more art. Try to plan an art project for when you are on holiday – on your own or as a team effort with family and friends. There will be more free time and maybe some new materials to find.

- Set yourself the task to make something new on a regular basis. Could you do it daily, weekly, monthly? If you tell friends and family about your plan, you are more likely to stick to it.

- If something succeeds, try making it again, but this time doing something different. Make it bigger or smaller; work faster and slower; take more care and then less care. Keep challenging yourself.

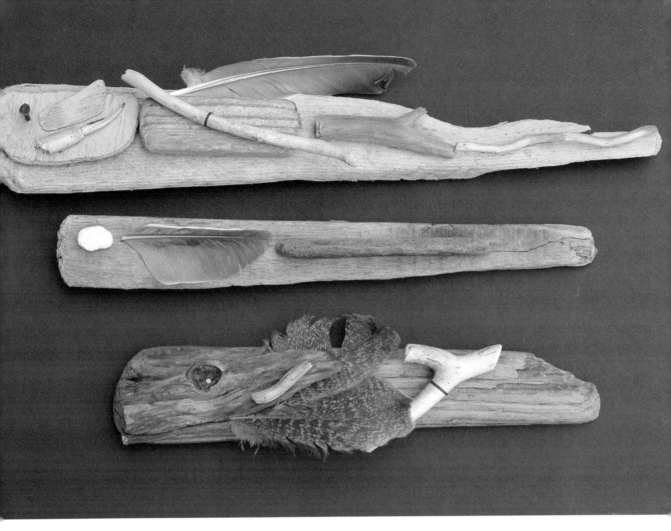

- Follow artists you have learned about in this book, via their websites, blogs, and by visiting galleries and exhibitions.

- Look for examples in museums of objects made with found, natural materials, collect postcards, or draw and write about them. Try your local museum too, however small it may be; you might be pleasantly surprised at what you will find.

- Keep a journal and sketchbook to record your ideas, thoughts and memories.

- Don't worry about making something that will last forever. Enjoy it while it lasts and then make another!

Above *Finished driftwood fish (see the project on p.34).*

Suppliers

The tools and materials you will need to buy are simple and easily available from good craft shops, DIY stores and online stores.

- -

AMAZON
An online store for craft books, some art and craft materials, small adhesive magnets, and tools.
www.amazon.com / www.amazon co.uk

AXMINSTER TOOL CENTRE
Shops in the UK and an online store. It is worth just having a look at the catalogue as it is so comprehensive. Good for general tools, including litter picker and pick-up tools, secateurs, knives, wax and oils, and books.
www.axminster.co.uk

HOBBYCRAFT
Stores in the UK and an online store. Ideal for glue, Trimits waxed linen thread in packets of 22 metres (72 feet), beeswax in a holder, and general craft supplies.
www.hobbycraft.co.uk

IKEA
Stores worldwide but may not sell smaller items online. Ideal for inexpensive box frames (extra deep frame) and display ideas.
www.ikea.com

JOHN LEWIS
Stores throughout the UK and online shopping including overseas deliveries. Ideal for craft supplies and jewellery fixings.
www.johnlewis.com

MERCHANT AND MILLS
An online store and stockists of general haberdashery around the world including Britain, Europe, North America and Japan. Their products are high quality with stylish vintage packaging.
http://merchantandmills.com

PAPERCHASE
A good range of craft materials online including self-adhesive magnets. There are stores throughout the UK, Europe (Republic of Ireland, Netherlands and Denmark) and the Middle East.
www.paperchase.co.uk

Further Reading

BOOKS

Atavar, M. 2009, *How To Be An Artist*, Kiosk Publishing, Australia.
An absorbing and motivating book packed full of useful tips on how to become an artist. My first choice of book to take to a desert island.

Costantino, M. 2010, *The Knot Handbook*, Kerswell Books Ltd.
A complete guide to tying and using knots with clear photography.

Cutler, C., Russell, T., and Walters, M. 2007, *The Illustrated Encyclopedia of Trees of the World*, Lorenz Books, Leicester.
An illustrated identification guide to 1000 trees from around the world.

Danks, F. and Schofield, J. 2010, *Make it Wild!: 101 Things to Make and Do Outdoors*, Frances Lincoln, London.
A book to encourage young people to experiment outside with a huge range of ideas and projects.

Dean, A. 1998, Natural Creativity: *Exploring and Using Nature's Raw Materials to Craft Simple, Functional and Attractive Objects,* M. Evans & Co Inc, Hertfordshire.
A book for all ages, encouraging creativity using the simple materials found in nature.

Gabriel, S. and Goymer, S. 1991, *The Complete Book of Basketry Techniques*, David & Charles, Newton Abbot, Devon.
A clear guide to basketry including selecting materials, tools and using a range of techniques.

Harding, S. and Waltener, S. 2012, *Practical Basketry Techniques*, Bloomsbury Publishing, London.
An introduction to all types of basket making with clear instructions and excellent photography.

Innes, M. 1993, *Country Craft Compendium*, Conran Octopus, London.
An easy-to-read selection of craft projects.

Legg, B. 2008, *Jewellery from Natural Materials*, A & C Black Publishers Ltd (Bloomsbury Publishing), London.
A beautifully illustrated and easy-to-follow book, guiding readers through six varied jewellery projects.

McGovern, U. 2008, *Lost Crafts: Rediscovering Traditional Skills*, Chambers, London.
A celebration of traditional skills such as quilting and dry-stone walling.

Mofield Mallow, J. 2010, *Pine Needle Basketry: From Forest Floor to Finished Project*, Lark Books, Broadway Asheville, NC.
A guide to making coiled pine needle baskets.

North House Folk School 2007, *Celebrating Birch: The Lore, Art, and Craft of an Ancient Tree*, Fox Chapel Publishing, E. Petersburg, PA.
An in-depth study of all aspects of the Northern birch, including biology, legends and craft projects.

Sterry, P. 2008, Collins *Complete Guide to British Trees: A photographic guide to every common species*, Collins, London.
One example of numerous guides to British trees, with background information on each one.

Stobart, J. 2011, *Extraordinary Sketchbooks: Inspiring Examples from Artists, Designers, Students and Enthusiasts*, A & C Black Publishers Ltd (Bloomsbury Publishing), London.
An inspiring book covering the personal sketchbooks of a number of artists and showing the importance of recording ideas.

Vaughan, S. 1994, *Handmade Baskets from Nature's Colourful Materials*, Search Press, Tunbridge Wells, Kent.
An introduction to basket making using materials found in the hedgerow.

FILM

The Wrecking Season 2004, motion picture, Boatshed Films. Distributed by Boatshed Films and the BBC, directed by Jane Darke, written by Nick Darke.
An extraordinarily inspiring film of a day in the life of a beachcomber on the North Cornwall coast.

MAGAZINES

www.craftcouncil.org/about/magazine
American Craft Magazine, published by American Craft Council, an award-winning bi-monthly magazine.

www.craftanddesign.net
Craft and Design Magazine, published bi-monthly.

www.craftscouncil.org.uk
Crafts Magazine, published bi-monthly by the Craft Council, England.

WEBSITES
ART IDEAS AND ACTIVITIES
www.how-to-be-an-artist.com
An immensely encouraging and enjoyable website and book to encourage creativity.

www.knowitall.org/naturalstate/index.cfm
'The Natural State' is a North American project exploring how artists use natural materials in their work with activities, teacher's resources and artist information.

www.motherearthnews.com/modern-homesteading/useful knots
A useful, easy-to-follow guide on how to tie knots.

www.naturedetectives.org.uk/art
The children's activities section of The Woodland Trust.

www.natureskills.com/survival/birch-bark-basket
Educational North American website teaching practical skills connected to the countryside, including this birch bark basket exercise.

GALLERY ARTISTS
www.scottishbasketmakerscircle.org/annaking
Anna King: Artist

www.carolinesharp.co.uk
Caroline Sharp: Artist and landscape architect

www.chrisdrury.co.uk
Chris Drury: Land artist

www.kategilliland.com
Kate Gilliland: Jewellery designer

www.devondriftwooddesigns.com
Karen Miller: Driftwood artist

www.kirstyelsondesigns.co.uk
Kirsty Elson: Artist

www.lizziefarey.co.uk
Lizzie Farey: Artist and designer maker

www.marianbijlenga.com
Marian Bijlenga: Fibre artist

www.lens-scape.co.uk
Terry Davies: Landscape photographer

www.sarahhoodjewelry.com
Sarah Hood: Jewellery artist

www.stellaharding.co.uk
Stella Harding: Artist and basket maker

www.susannabauer.com
Susanna Bauer: Artist

www.susievaughan.co.uk
Susie Vaughan: Basket maker

www.wycliffestutchbury.co.uk
Wycliffe Stutchbury: Artist

ART ORGANISATIONS, GALLERIES AND MUSEUMS
www.basketassoc.org
The Basket Makers Association has information on makers, workshops and exhibitions in England.

www.basketry.ac.uk
Website for the 2011 exhibition 'Basketry – Making Human Nature', organised by the Sainsbury Centre for the Visual Arts, with a broad and international context for basket making as well as information on contemporary artists and educational activities.

www.britishmuseum.org
The British Museum in London has objects made of natural materials from around the world, particularly from Africa and the Americas, on display. Many can be viewed online.

www.craftact.org.au
Craft ACT: Craft and Design Centre in Canberra, Australia is one of a number of centres for contemporary craft in Australia which run exhibitions and events supporting local contemporary craft and design practitioners through membership and other activities.

www.craftscouncil.org.uk
The Crafts Council of England has information on craft exhibitions, events and a directory of makers.

www.craftcouncil.org
The American Crafts Council, based in Minneapolis, has information on American artists, exhibitions and events.

www.craftinamerica.org
A comprehensive site dedicated to the preservation and celebration of

the American Craft Movement with links to artists, exhibitions, film and video.

www.object.com.au
Object is Australia's leading centre for design, based in New South Wales, Australia, celebrating Australian artists through exhibitions and education.

www.prm.ox.ac.uk
The Pitt Rivers Museum in Oxford, UK, founded in 1884, contains a vast collection of around 300,000 archaeological and ethnographic objects from around the world, many made of natural materials. A good selection can be viewed online.

www.scottishbasketmakerscircle. org
The Scottish Basket Makers Group promotes basket making in Scotland through exhibitions, courses and fairs.

ORGANISATIONS CONCERNED WITH THE ENVIRONMENT
www.arkive.org
Films and photographs of the world's endangered species in a centralised digital library.

www.communityforest.org.uk/ aboutenglandsforests.htm
England's 15 community forests are social and economic regeneration projects located near large urban areas.

www.field-studies-council.org
The Field Studies Council is a UK charity started in 1943, promoting understanding of the environment, with a section on arts and crafts.

www.forestry.gov.uk/forest/INFO-6ZFMZ
The links between health and the wooded environment in particular are explored in depth in this 'Woods For Health' Strategy 2009 by the Forestry Commission, Scotland and NHS Health Scotland.

www.goodbeachguide.co.uk
Guide to the best beaches in the UK.

www.hedgerows.co.uk
The Hedgerow Trust is a charitable organisation that aims to preserve hedgerows offering education and advice.

www.kew.org
The Royal Botanic Gardens at Kew is home to glasshouses, gardens and plants from around the world, as well as art exhibitions.

www.mcsuk.org/what_we_do
UK Marine Conservation Society for the protection of the seas, shores and wildlife.

www.nationalforest.org
An awarding-winning national project to transform 200 square miles in Central England into forest. The website has information and ideas for health, communities and education.

www.nationaltrust.org.uk
As well as historic properties, the National Trust protects countryside locations too and offers guided walks and arts activities.

www.naturalengland.org. uk/ourwork/enjoying/ countrysidecode
Natural England promotes people, places and nature with health walks and a section on the UK Countryside Code.

www.nps.gov/index.htm
The official site for the North American National Park Service with beautiful photography, ideas for art and education and information on the parks.

www.ramblers.org.uk
An organisation that promotes access to the countryside and provides information on walking, helping you locate walking groups near you.

www.slowmovement.com
The Slow Movement encourages a more balanced lifestyle and connections to locality and communities.

www.woodlandtrust.org.uk
UK woodland conservation charity with information on species identification, facts, ideas and links to your local woodland.

www.worldparksday.com/world-parks-day
Parks for Life, an international initiative created by the International Parks and Green Space Alliance (IUPGSA).

Glossary

Acorn cup Woody base in which the acorn sits; the nut of the oak tree.

Anti-oxidant Substances in our food that can prevent or slow down damage to our bodies from the damaging free radicals produced when our body cells use oxygen.

Assembly A basketry technique in which materials are constructed, not woven. More often associated with contemporary basket making.

Bark The outer protective layers of trees, which overlay the wood and grow with the tree.

Basketry An ancient handmade craft in which materials are intertwined using various techniques to make functional and decorative objects.

Beach litter Human-created waste and rubbish that has washed up on the coastline. Also known as tidewrack.

Beeswax Natural wax from honeybees, used for a wide variety of purposes and purchased in tins or as solid sticks.

Bevelled Sloping edge of an object, created by sanding or shaving.

Bight A knot-making term referring to the loop or slack part of a rope when it is folded over.

Box frame A picture frame with extra space between the board and the glass, making it ideal for framing three-dimensional material.

Bradawl Small tool, similar to a straight screwdriver, used to make an indentation ready for the screw or nail to be inserted.

Coiling Basketry technique in which a length of material is coiled in a spiral action by stitching it to the layer beneath.

Cordage Refers to all rope, string and ties of any thickness.

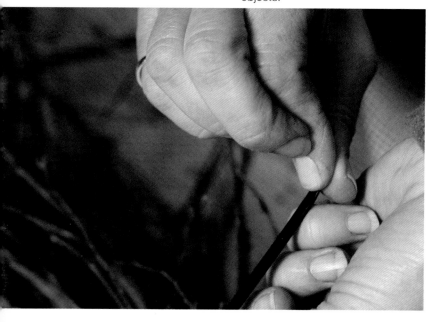

Cuttlebone The hard internal structure of the cuttlefish, used for buoyancy and frequently found washed up on beaches. It is rich in calcium and can be given to domestic pets and birds to chew.

Driftwood Wood that has been washed up on the shore by wind or waves.

Ecology The study of plants, animals and their environment.

Ecosystem A network between organisms and their environment.

Evergreen A plant that has leaves throughout the year.

Forage To wander in search of something.

Glycerine A thick, clear liquid that absorbs moisture and is soluble in water. Used in the food industry, it presents no hazards to the user.

Gumnut Hard and woody fruit from the eucalyptus tree.

Haberdashery A shop selling sewing items such as buttons, needles and threads.

Indigenous or native Belonging to or originating from a particular place.

Jute twine Twine or string made of natural jute fibres, usually brown in colour.

Lenticel Thin, dark slits in the surface of some types of tree bark, which allows for the passing of gases.

Linseed oil Yellowish oil from the seeds of the flax plant. The oil is used as a wood finisher. It is edible and presents no hazards to the user.

Marine litter Human-created waste and rubbish adrift in the sea.

Natural materials Materials that are part of the natural world and not made by man.

Nature conservation area An area of land protected by law.

Razor clams Long, rectangular shell which lives under coarse sand on the shoreline.

Scavenge To search for salvageable material.

Shuttlecock Open, conical cone used to play badminton.

Shoal Large group of fish or marine animals.

Slate Fine grained, often grey rock.

Stake and strand Basketry technique in which horizontal elements are woven around and through upright stakes.

Tendrils Coiled, spring-like leaf or stem used by climbing plants as support, wrapping around the host.

Toggle Here refers to an elongated button, used to hold two items together.

Twining Basketry technique in which two horizontal elements (wefts) are woven around stationary uprights (warp) with a turn in between.

Upright Vertical element in basket making around which materials can be woven or twined. Also known as stakes.

Vine Trailing or climbing plants such as ivy, grape and clematis.

Waxed thread Thread which has been impregnated with wax so it will stay firmly in position.

Wrecker Someone who collects objects washed up on the shoreline, also known as a beachcomber.

Appendix: exercise in adaptive learning

Materials you might want to collect and use

- Feathers
- Sycamore seeds
- Pine needles
- Driftwood
- Pebbles
- Shells
- Cuttlefish bone
- Thorns
- Twigs
- Branches
- Bark
- Leaves
- Reeds
- Acorn cups

Techniques to experiment with (use your own ideas as well)

- Twisting
- Tying
- Folding
- Binding
- Wrapping
- Weaving
- Plaiting
- Slotting
- Knitting
- Bunching
- Stitching
- Cutting
- Knotting
- Slicing

Adaptive learning is a way of making art, researched and championed by sculptor, craftsman and applied ecologist Dr Tim Willey. You can read about his methods in more depth on his website: www.timwilley.com.

This approach starts with trying out a range of simple actions on your selected materials, but adapting the plan as you go along depending on your results. First of all, gather different materials that appeal to you – interesting and intriguing items that you have picked up and would like to use in some way.

Then take a list of 'actions' (see ideas in the list) and spend a few hours trying these out, one by one, on your materials, and see what results. You will discover what the materials can do and achieve some great results that would not have happened had you followed a rigid plan.

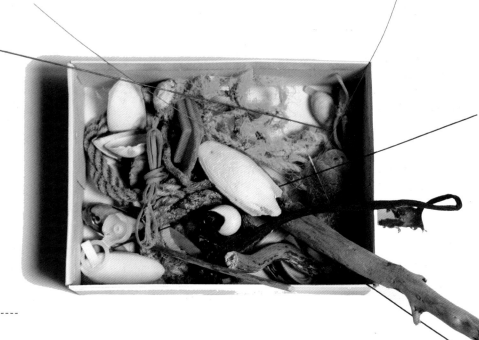

Index

Acknowledgements

Above: Wycliffe Stutchbury, Quercus Robur 5, English Oak, 2010. Timber from dismantled fruit cage, 172 x 31 cm (68½ x 12 in). 'My compositions from fallen and forgotten timber are studies in the narrative beauty of wood.' Photo: Wycliffe Stutchbury.

With many heartfelt thanks to Alison Stace for having such a brilliant idea for the book, to Kate Sherington at Bloomsbury Publishing for her great support, and to all the many artists and makers who have generously allowed their work to be reproduced here.

The book would not have been possible without the commitment and enthusiasm of photographer Paul Tupman.

Thanks also to the many friends who gave freely of their endless interest, advice and knowledge, as well as the odd bird's nest and supply of feathers. Emma Barnes of Native Forestry, Sarah Spencer, Robin and Lizzie Raines, Dr Tim Willey, Caroline Barnes, Jocelyn Dodd, Deirdre Figueiredo and Helen Juffs. Finally, thanks to my family for their support, especially Dan for his unerring commitment to foraging and beachcombing.

DISCLAIMER

Every effort has been made to ensure the accuracy of the information and the safety of the projects in this book, but neither author nor publisher can be held responsible for any resulting injury, damage or loss to persons or property. Follow all health and safety guidelines and seek additional advice if required.